The Church and the Hour

The Church and the Hour

Reflections of a Socialist Churchwoman

By

Vida D. Scudder, A.M.

Wipf & Stock
PUBLISHERS
Eugene, Oregon

Wipf and Stock Publishers
199 W 8th Ave, Suite 3
Eugene, OR 97401

The Church and the Hour
By Scudder, Vida D.
ISBN 13: 978-1-57910-547-1
ISBN 10: 1-57910-547-5
Publication date 12/22/2000
Previously published by E. P. Dutton & Co., 1917

PREFACE

ALTHOUGH this little book is entitled Papers by a Socialist Churchwoman, there is no discussion of socialism in it. This is because the author does not feel that the Church at large should be called upon to commit itself to any Ism, or special set of economic doctrines. She does not see, to be candid, how an intelligent Christian can help being a socialist. But that is her narrowness. She is obliged to confess that many devout and able minds do not embrace the creed so dear to her; and she is not concerned in this place with propaganda, but with considering the distinctive work and function of the Church as it is. If she is privately convinced that such action and attitude as this book calls for will lead all communicants ultimately to the socialist position, that is her own affair and might form the subject of another book. Her effort has been to pierce below controversy; to be very practical; above all, to suggest only what everyone on reflection must agree that honest discipleship to the Son of Mary under modern conditions would involve.

It may be noticed that some of the papers strike a more pessimistic and critical note than others in regard to the probability of the Church's furnishing effective social leadership. That is because these papers were written at intervals during the last five years, and circumstances have caused the prospect to appear now brighter, now darker. That the Introduction which is the latest written should also be the most optimistic, may be of good augury.

CONTENTS

	PAGE
PREFACE	v
INTRODUCTION	1
THE ALLEGED FAILURE OF THE CHURCH TO MEET THE SOCIAL EMERGENCY. PAPER PRESENTED AT THE CHURCH CONGRESS IN NORFOLK, VA., MAY, 1916	40
THE CHURCH'S OPPORTUNITY. (Reprinted from *The Churchman*, 1913)	74
TWO LETTERS TO THE MASSES. (Reprinted from *The Masses*, Dec., 1915, Feb., 1916)	95
WHY DOES NOT THE CHURCH TURN SOCIALIST? (Reprinted from *The Coming Nation*, 1913)	103
A PLEA FOR SOCIAL INTERCESSION. (Reprinted from *The Churchman*)	119
THE SIGN OF THE SON OF MAN	131

The Church and the Hour

Christian democracy applied to industry means the development of coöperative relations to the fullest possible extent. The Church should therefore clearly teach the principle of the fullest possible coöperative control and ownership of industry and the natural resources upon which industry depends, in order that men may be spurred to develop the methods that shall express this principle.

Report of the Commission on the Church and Social Service to the Quadrennial Meeting of the Federal Council of the Churches of Christ in America. December, 1916.

The Church and the Hour

PAPERS BY A SOCIALIST CHURCHWOMAN

INTRODUCTION

I

THE papers presented in this little book were written for widely varying publics. The longer were contributed to Church papers or delivered before Church audiences; some of the shorter were printed in the socialist press and addressed to people who have no point of contact with the Church. But all had one object: to promote better understanding between the religious world which fears social revolution, and the unchurched world of radical passion which desires it.

These two worlds are nearer each other than is commonly supposed or than either realizes. Among radicals, the irrepressible hunger for spiritual experience stirs here and there unmistakably. And this in spite of bitter abuse and scorn lavished not on Christ Himself but on His followers. It is all very well to assert that "The Church is Judas Iscariot," that creeds are dead and that no cult of an Oriental god can solve modern problems. One may gather such assertions by the handful from the pages of the radical press. But through the defiance of the authors runs more and more a note of doubt. For the truth is that creeds are not dead but very much alive, that the "Oriental god" is still to countless men the one Master of the world's salvation, and that the churches, akin rather to Peter than to Judas, are almost awake to the peril in which they have been of betraying their Lord. Their vast reservoirs of social power have been long ice-bound. But the ice is breaking, the waters begin to move. It is not beyond hope, that soon these waters may be released, to flow forth, at the moment when the need of the world is greatest, in streams that shall be for the healing of the nations.

Introduction 3

The social awakening of the churches is the great fact which this little book would signal, and in its modest way would further.

It is full time that the critics of the Church, — and they are many, including some of her most loyal children,—should become aware of the advanced position which various official Christian groups are now taking at last on questions concerning social justice. From one point of view, to be sure, official statements count for nothing. If too far ahead of the public conscience, they become inert formulæ, and formulæ not translated into life are the ancient curse of religion. On the other hand, however, if the Church finds no corporate expression for the restlessness and compunction that consume Christian hearts to-day, she will soon deserve the contempt or indifference which she is sure to inspire. The Spirit ever works at first secretly, kindling in the wills of the faithful fires that cannot be concealed; but in due time these fires light on the altar of the Church flames that shall illumine the world.

Not very long ago, Christians who felt the revolutionary implications of their faith looked in vain to the churches for any encouragement or endorsement. To draw out the social significance of the Gospels, to define Christian duty in terms of industrial justice for an industrial age, was a task wholly neglected and desperately necessary. As recently as the time of Maurice and Kingsley, it was attempted by English Christianity only through sweeping generalities if at all, and these noble pioneers were distrusted by religious authorities and silenced in religious circles. As lately as the time of Phillips Brooks, the task could be ignored by a great spiritual leader. But it cannot be ignored any longer, and the power to rest in generalities is past. Concrete and stinging must be the application of Christian ideals made by the Church to modern civilization and modern Christian lives. The last years have taught all who watch Europe that there are no heights of sacrifice to which humanity will refuse to rise if the summons sounds authentic.

But if the Church has failed to offer any social leadership through official channels, at least the voice of great churchmen pleading

Introduction 5

for justice has never been silent down the Christian ages:

"So destructive a passion is avarice that to grow rich without injustice is impossible. . . . But what if a man succeeded to his father's inheritance? Then he received what has been gathered by injustice. For . . . of the many who were before him somebody must unjustly have taken and enjoyed the goods of others . . . because God left the earth free to all alike. Why then if it is common, have you so many acres of land, and your neighbor has not a portion of it?"—Henry George is not speaking: that is St. Chrysostom.

"It will be objected to holding goods in common that governments will perish because no one cares to preserve common property. But no, if that law were in force, states would be most excellently preserved. . . . For goods are to be cared for in proportion to their excellence. Now goods held in common are the best of all,—therefore, they must be cared for most perfectly." That is not a modern syndicalist utterance, it is Wyclif in his youth, writing his *De Dominio Civile*.

Quotations equally telling might be multiplied from age to age. But statements bearing the stamp of ecclesiastical authority are harder to seek. An outstanding fact is the Encyclical of Pope Leo XIII, Rerum Novarum, dating from 1891. It reads mildly enough now, but it was considered at the time to be very socialistic in tendency, and it does call for a revised concept of Christian duty, in the light of the modern economic situation. From the dawn of the twentieth century, expressions of social faith slowly appear; so that some day, history may narrate the capture of the modern Church by a social Christian ideal. Among English-speaking Christians, the first striking group-utterance of the century was perhaps that of the Lambeth Conference of 1908. It sounds rather faint beside St. Chrysostom, but is good as far as it goes:

"What is now needed is . . . groups of Christian men and women in every place determined to make it their aim to bring the sense of justice and righteousness which is common to Christianity and to Democracy, to bear upon the matters of every-day life in trade, in society, and wherever their influence extends: and to stir up public opinion on behalf of the removal of wrong wherever it may be found, thus making an earnest endeavor to share in the transforming work of Christianity for their brethren and companions' sake." It would be interesting to know to whom this statement was due.

In this country, viewing all organized Christianity together, the first impressive landmark is the platform adopted by the Federal Council of Churches in Chicago, 1912:

"The churches must stand:

"1. For equal rights and complete justice for all men in all stations of life.

"2. For the protection of the family, by the single standard of purity, uniform divorce laws, proper regulation of marriage, and proper housing.

"3. For the fullest possible development for every child, especially by the provision of proper education and recreation.

"4. For the abolition of child labor.

"5. For such regulation of the conditions of toil for women as shall safeguard the physical and moral health of the community.

"6. For the abatement and prevention of poverty.

"7. For the protection of the individual and society from the social, economic, and moral waste of the liquor traffic.

"8. For the conservation of health.

"9. For the protection of the worker from dangerous machinery, occupational diseases, and mortality.

"10. For the right of all men to the opportunity for self-maintenance, for safeguarding this right against encroachments of every kind, and for the protection of workers from the hardships of enforced unemployment.

"11. For suitable provision for the old age of the workers, and for those incapacitated by injury.

"12. For the right of employees and employers alike to organize; and for adequate means of conciliation and arbitration in industrial disputes.

"13. For a release from employment one day in seven.

"14. For the gradual and reasonable reduction of the hours of labor to the lowest practicable point, and for that degree of

Introduction 9

leisure for all which is a condition of the highest human life.

"15. For a living wage as a minimum in every industry, and for the highest wage that each industry can afford.

"16. For a new emphasis upon the application of Christian principles to the acquisition and use of property, and for the most equitable division of the product of industry that can ultimately be devised."

That document certainly registers a great advance on the statement of the Lambeth Conference. It is the work of minds trained not only to social emotion but to practical social thinking, and it is cognizant of specific modern issues. Claims as extreme as any radical could make are interspersed among definite points which, taken together, remind one of the platform of the Progressive Party, —a document, it may incidentally be said, modeled if report speak true on this very program. "Equal rights and complete justice for all men," "The abatement and prevention of poverty," "The most equitable division of the product of industry that can ultimately be devised" . . . the words have a vigorous ring, and they are redeemed from the suggestion of verbiage without vision, by the practical propositions in regard to child-labor, the minimum wage, pensions, the right to organize, the reduction of working hours "to the lowest practicable point," and the like. It is an admirable program. It sets a mark to which many of the separate churches have not yet begun to attain.

In the quadrennial meeting of the same Council, held in St. Louis, Dec. 1916, this program was reaffirmed, with a preamble well worth quoting:

STATEMENT OF SOCIAL FAITH

The Federal Council of the Churches of Christ in America expresses again the deepening conviction that the scope of the gospel and the program of the churches must include the creation on earth of a Christian civilization, organized upon the ethical teachings and controlled by the spirit of Jesus Christ.

In addition to the unquestioned historic mission and work of Christianity with the individual, we understand this to involve certain great social accomplishments; that

Introduction 11

among these are: the abolishment of war; the transformation of the dangerous commercial rivalries of the nations into a just and brotherly coöperation; the coming together on terms of equality and justice of capitalist, employer, workers, and the consuming public in brotherly coöperative effort, and the shifting of industry from off its basis of profits upon that of human welfare; the lifting of the women of the world to a position of freedom and equality with the men of the world; the destruction of the curse of strong drink; the control of the infectious diseases which afflict humanity; the control of the vices of the race; the removal of the handicap of poverty from submerged millions of people of all nations; the uplift of backward races and their freedom from the permanent and enforced domination of more powerful peoples; the extension of democracy throughout the earth, and the development of its efficiency and honesty, with the supreme emphasis upon the spiritual values of human life. Many of these objectives, perhaps all of them in their wider reaches are the work of generations; but they are within the power of human effort when sustained and scientifically organized, and henceforth they are to be ever before the churches. They call for faith and consecrated endeavor on an unprecedented scale.

The whole report is full of practical and pertinent suggestions.

Among the churches, the Anglican or Protestant-Episcopal,—a body rather shy of its own name, but at present legally known by the latter title—has usually been reckoned one of the most instinctively conservative and aristocratic. But the last two General Conventions have taken action which at least partially exonerates it from this accusation. The Convention meets triennially, with two Houses, a House of Bishops and a Lower House of Clergy and Lay Deputies, and it is the official organ of the Church. In 1910, the Convention endorsed the appointment of a Social Service Commission. In 1913, this Commission was actually appointed, and got to work, being confirmed in 1916. In the meantime, local Social Service Commissions were appointed in many provinces, dioceses, and parishes, until the organization of this

Introduction 13

new activity is on the way to become as thorough as that of the missionary activities of the Church, with which, in the mind of members of the Commission, it should run parallel. The Joint Commission has been occupied largely in aiding the creation of this machinery and in preparing itself to coöperate with the other commissions; it has published some excellent literature, it conducted an effective educational campaign during the Convention of 1916, and it is preparing conferences on a large scale, for the consideration of economic and social problems from the strictly Christian point of view, to be held in different sections of the country. Its chief aim is not the undertaking of practical reforms, which must in the nature of things lie outside its scope, but the social education of each communicant and each child of the Church; and the reception of its study courses and pamphlets shows how ready the Church and its members are to welcome just such work.

But the Convention did more than appoint a Commission. In both 1913 and 1916 it took a definite stand on social fundamentals. In 1913, the following Resolution was passed:

WHEREAS, The moral and spiritual welfare of the people demands that the highest possible standard of living should everywhere be maintained and that all conduct of industry should emphasize the search for such higher and more human forms of organization as will genuinely elicit the personal definite stake in the system of production to which the worker's life is given; and

WHEREAS, Injustice and disproportionate inequality as well as misunderstanding, prejudice, and mutual distrust as between employer and employee are widespread in our social and industrial life to-day:

THEREFORE, BE IT RESOLVED, The House of Bishops concurring, that we, the members of the General Convention of the Protestant Episcopal Church, do hereby affirm that the Church stands for the ideal of social justice, and that it demands the achievement of a social order in which the social cause of poverty and the gross human waste of the present order shall be eliminated, and in which every member shall have a just return for what he produces, a free opportunity for self-development, and a fair share in all the gains of

Introduction 15

progress. And since such a social order can only be achieved progressively by the efforts of men and women who in the spirit of Christ put the common welfare above private gain, the Church calls upon every communicant, clerical and lay, seriously to take part in the study of the complex conditions under which we are called upon to live, and so to act that the present prejudice and injustice may be supplanted by mutual understanding, sympathy, and just dealing, and the ideal of a thoroughgoing democracy may be fully realized in our land.

That is advanced, in its outspoken repudiation of *Laisser-faire*, and its assertion that spiritual welfare demands the highest possible standard of living,—an assertion which sentimental and other-worldly Christians are always loath to admit, and which indeed if literally and individually applied might carry us into strange regions. It is also fine in maintaining that disproportionate inequality obtains in social and industrial life to-day, and in its statement that the Church demands a social order in which the social cause of poverty shall be eliminated. If Christians at large would only recognize the responsibility of religion *per se* to eliminate the social cause of poverty, instead of claiming too often that religion has nothing to do with the matter, the struggle for justice would be half won.

But when the Resolution passes from general statements to definite recommendations, it betrays a generation still in the fog. The non-committal appeal, or instruction, to communicants, is a decided drop from the first part of the statement. They are asked chiefly to study conditions: also, so to act that justice and sympathy may be promoted and the ideal of democracy be realized. It is true that study must precede action and that the first step onward is to create a right temper in Christian people, but one may doubt whether these general adjurations, excellent as they are, would make any difference to the readers of them. Certainly, communicants in 1917 ought to be and are ready for more definite guidance.

Such guidance they get, in respect both to thought and action, from a Resolution passed at the General Convention in the autumn of 1916. It is simpler and briefer than the statements hitherto quoted, and it omits all denunciation of the present system, as well as any attempt to formulate the ultimate principles of a Christian social order. It is addressed to the Church as it is, not to the Church as radicals want it to be; for as has felicitously been said, the Church is not a radical body, but a *bourgeois* body touched with compunction. But in spite of the quiet tone of the Resolution, it implies the necessity for profound change as thoroughly as does the Resolution of 1913; it cuts deeper into the matter of private conduct and starts in at least on the difficult and unusual task of suggesting to Christian people precise points at which through their personal action social reformation might begin:

BE IT RESOLVED, That the service of the community and the welfare of the workers, not primarily private profits, should be the aim of every industry and its justification; and that the Church should seek to keep this aim constantly before the mind of the public; and that Christians as individuals are under the obligation on the one hand conscientiously to scrutinize the sources of their income, and on the other hand to give moral support and prayer to every just effort to secure fair conditions and regular employment for wage-earners and the extension of true democracy to industrial matters.

Production for use and not for private profit is the very nucleus of socialist theory. Social revolution is not too strong a phrase to describe the cleavage that would ensue between our present methods and a civilization governed by that central principle in its economics. To call on the Church constantly to keep this transformation before the public mind is to place a new responsibility on every clergyman and communicant. As for the command that Christians scrutinize the sources of their incomes, it does not at first sound very drastic. St. Chrysostom and the socialist local will agree in going further and telling us that we ought not to have any incomes at all. Perhaps, however, if we scrutinize sources thoroughly and conscientiously, there may not in the long run be much

Introduction 19

income left. If Christian people in general should discover by any chance that the sources of income under the present system can rarely bear scrutiny, when exposed to the flashlight of conscience, they may decide that the present system has got to go.

"Moral support and prayer" for every just effort of the wage-earners or others to secure fair conditions for labor is a suggestion which cuts at the center. What Christendom really prays for, it will work for and will gain. How much praying is the habit of Christian hearts as a regular part of their religious duty, when strikes are in progress, one wonders? And what about moral support? Too often, Church people behave as if industrial or legislative struggles were none of their concern. Parochial activities, Sunday-Schools, Girls' Friendly, Missions,—these are their concern and the concern of the Church. The other matters are out of her province, and indifference masked in humility declines to hold an opinion about them. All this should now be changed. If people obey the summons of the Church, as expressed both in 1913 and 1916, they can no longer easily assume that it is none of their responsibility to make up their minds about the rights in a labor war. It is their Christian business to attend to such matters, to have opinions when possible, to take sides, and to support the struggle of and for the workers, whenever they shall consider it just,—not otherwise,—with their sympathy and with their prayers. The last phrase, about the extension of democracy to industry, may help them a little in this difficult matter of forming an opinion. It affords a guiding principle, in the light of which the decision where to throw one's sympathy in concrete cases becomes easier. This Resolution of 1916 was enthusiastically and unanimously adopted by the Bishops, and endorsed by the Lower House. It is not the expression of a conservative-minded body, it is the expression of brave men.

In the light of these statements, it is no longer possible to complain that the Churches are silent. The social feeling of individual Christians may still so outstrip any corporate Church expression that it commands a new horizon; but this is rarely true of their

Introduction

social action. If Church members would pursue the course of conduct implied in these recent formulæ, they would make their Christianity a visible fact, forced on the recognition of everyone. They would live in a mountain city, set on high for all to see as their Master pictured them, instead of settling down, contentedly to all appearance, as they mostly do now, among other folk in the sordid cities of the plain.

"He that hath an ear, let him hear what the Spirit saith unto the Churches."

II

There are two interesting points in connection with these formulæ. The first is, that in all of them, the attack on the existing order is scrupulously from the moral, not the economic end. The last Resolution of the Episcopal Convention was even commended by the New York *Times* on this account! Even the program of the Federal Council, though it treads debatable ground, treads it with such cautious steps that it would be hard for any

Christian to disagree with its practical demands. This reticence is wise. For it is a pity that the Church should take controversial positions with which honest Christians can disagree, when there are so many positions out of the reach of legitimate controversy which are nevertheless quite revolutionary in character! Such honest Christians ought not to have their freedom of thinking violated by *ex-cathedra* pronouncements from the Church. To be allowed to think foolishly, if we must think foolishly to think honestly, is a prerogative hardly won, which the race must very jealously guard: all of us need the protection of it sometimes, and to deny that sacred right leads straight to the Inquisition. In this new function of social guidance on which the Church is seemingly entering, she needs to practice very delicate discrimination. To get up a party which shall fight to gain the endorsement of the Church for this measure or that program is an attractive short-cut to social Christianity, but it is a short-cut that leads to By-Ends' Meadows and will end by plunging the Church into the morass of politics.

Socialists claim, and rightly, that the lack of

Introduction 23

thinking in economic terms is fatal to a sense for reality, and every Christian is under orders to learn how to think in these terms. But the business of the Church as a Church is to translate them into Christian ethics. This is good strategics; it creates a far more salutary annoyance to press home the disturbing truths to which Christians are nominally committed by virtue of their allegiance, in language which no Christian can challenge, than to deal in alien technicalities. In the statements just quoted, it is hard to find anything which the Christian disciple could deny, short of making the fundamental assertion that the relations of men in this world are none of his business. This is why those statements are effective. Economic programs are necessary in their place, but one does not need to adopt the specious "dynamic" theory of the Church to see that this place is not in Church formulæ.

Nor does this opinion invite the Church to take refuge in evasive platitudes,—an easy alternative all too readily embraced on occasion by bishops and other clergy, not to speak of the laity. It means that the Church has a distinctive and difficult work to do. To probe to the quick, to trouble people, to sting them into courses of action that involve unconventionality, pluck, readiness for adventure,—that is her duty. But this sort of result is gained only by direct appeal to heart and conscience. Possibly the teaching of the Church, if it is sincere, must lead those who obey to share the fate of their Master, Who was pursued by the venomous enmity of the respectable classes of His day, and was finally executed as a criminal by the unanimous will of the religious and the secular authorities. That ought to suffice. Let the Church speak her own language. If bravely and consistently uttered, if faithfully obeyed, it will be found to correspond closely with economic theories quite at variance with those on which society now more or less uneasily reposes; and, under pressure from two diverse directions making for one same end, the world may find itself transformed.

The other point to notice about these statements is that the Church is not appealing especially to the working classes. She is not thinking in terms of class at all. What is in her mind is no movement pushed from behind by the sharp prong of economic distress, it is rather a general movement impelled by such single-hearted passion for justice as should be common to all people. And here again, her policy will discredit her in many radical minds. Those who cling to the Marxian belief that substantial progress is won only by the rebellion of the oppressed, will scorn the appeal to disinterested action. Nor are the Marxians alone. Whether one looks at nations or at classes, a widespread feeling that no group of men will ever act contrary to their own interests, and that the future of the world must be determined by balance of greeds, cuts the nerve of idealist effort. Some warm idealists are among those who distrust a general appeal. They too feel that the slow pressure of the working classes toward power is the one effective hope for freedom; and they think that the most useful thing for a lover of justice to do is to unclass himself and to throw in his lot with the proletarian struggle.

Now there is a misunderstanding here which needs to be cleared up.

It is true that this upward movement of men

seeking expansion and freedom is the most salient and inevitable fact of history. For the first sacred duty imposed on nations, on classes, on individuals, is the search for life's fulfillment. Fullness of life must precede any impulse toward sacrifice. Life must be whole before it can be offered; there was no mutilation of Our Lord's Body on the Cross. It was a perfect Humanity which there gave itself in an oblation full, perfect, and sufficient for the sins of the whole world.

And so, while the Church cannot endorse the crass forms of economic determinism, and will never yield to a materialistic interpretation of history, she is not debarred from warm sympathy with the class struggle. Far from being debarred from such sympathy, Christian people are called to it. So long as they can applaud the self-defense of a small nation, they cannot condemn the self-defense of a weak class. Beyond the fogs in which we grope, shines the fair intermittent vision of a non-resistant humanity; we look at it wistfully and honor those conscientious objectors who even now seek to walk in its light. But to invoke that vision when a big people

Introduction

tramples down a little people, is not yet within the compass of much Christian thought. Equally beyond that compass should be disapproval or indifference toward the fight of working-class groups to preserve or enlarge their liberties. Feeble girl garment-workers learning to stand together for their rights with the light of battle dawning in their eyes, respond to the rhythmic stress which is evolving life throughout the universe; they are part of the God-consciousness ever quickening in the clay. The struggle for freedom is righteous and religious, whether it be found in striking miner or in outraged nation, and Christian hearts must recognize in it the motions of the Lord and Giver of Life.

Yet this struggle, whether in the form of demand for better wages and hours, or for political independence, is on the lower range of human action, on the range of the natural life. The Church is one with nature, one it may almost be said with common sense, in approving it; but the Church as Church has no relation to it at all. For her business is with life on the higher level, the life regenerate. On this level she must teach, from this level she must appeal. Her distinctive song is not the *Marseillaise*, though she does not forbid her children to sing it; it is the *Vexilla Regis*. The Royal Banner under which her host advances against the host of evil, is the banner of the Cross.

Naturally, the world scoffs, nor can any one be surprised at its scepticism in face of the spectacle of history. Perhaps non-religious people may long have to remain bound in the chains of scepticism and economic determinism; perhaps the best they can share is the lower though holy enthusiasm of the fighters for freedom on the lower plane. None the less, the Church knows that the world is wrong. Hers is no cynic distrust, no pseudo-scientific fatalism. She is aware of a secret principle, working counter to the indrawing principle that claims and appropriates,—the outgoing principle that sacrifices and gives. The Church knows that man is the child of God by adoption and grace, and that he can rise to God-like action; for she has marked his brow with the Holy Sign. Baptismal Regeneration is a doctrine consigned to the rear of most Christian minds. If it means anything,

Introduction 29

it means a triumphant refutation of the determinist. It asserts that Christian folk can be appealed to *en masse*, to act on a supernatural level, where their private interest will yield instinctively and as a matter of course, to the general good.

The Church's faith in a regenerate humanity is not much in evidence just now. To regain it, she must descend into the depths of her most mystical convictions. If she can get even a wee mustard-seed measure of that faith, she can say to the mountains of class-greed and privilege, Be ye cast down and thrown into the sea. They would crumble away, those mountains, they would fall in crashing avalanche, down, down, till no vestige of them remained. Her opportunity and her power are unique, if she will greatly dare. Her belief that the whole body of Christian people coming under her jurisdiction can and must be raised to disinterested social action, makes her mistress of a province all her own. It is her distinctive contribution to the present crisis. So far, she has at best only reiterated what other right-minded bodies are saying, but it is inconceivable that she should pause there. Far from merely echoing approval of measures which secular agencies endorse, which even the Government in some cases begins to further, she might take the initiative. Her work is not to announce new economic theories, it is only incidentally to approve specific programs. It is to insist that her children sift theories uncompromisingly in the light of Christian idealism; it is above all to offer the incentive which shall draw men to try the Great Adventure of Christian living in terms of the new age.

III

The Church must not only call to action, she must show the way to it. And that is more difficult, for even honest eyes see such a tangle of paths! And the Hill of Calvary, from which the only true way reaches, rises very far from modern vision. But perhaps in these heart-rending days, eyes purged with tears are growing more able to discern it.

Two special phases of social consecration are demanded by the present crisis. The one concerns the private life of the individual, the other the group-life of the Christian community.

Introduction 31

As to the private life: in one direction, the Christian world has been sufficiently instructed. One would not dare say that it did its duty, but certainly unless it is deaf it knows where that duty lies. This is the direction of practical activity. Social Service is the word of the hour, and the constant message of the pulpit calls people to devote themselves to it. Optimism sees most people obeying the call. Nearly all serious-minded folk give a large portion of their spare time, not to amusement or self-culture, but to one of the multiform modern ways of promoting the Kingdom of God. If one sometimes wonders whether it was meant that this Kingdom should be promoted by sitting on committees, one crushes the unworthy thought. If a good deal of effort is amateurish and wasted, one renews one's faith that aim and effort are the really creative things. Splendid works are carried on effectively,—till one measures them against the need they try to meet. And better perhaps than all Church activities, is the other effect of the ideal of service: the socializing of the professions. In every pursuit, the motive of service can be made central. If it cannot, that is no pursuit for Christian men.

But beyond action, lie the more searching questions connected with fundamental attitude toward possessions, toward the world. And here each socially enlightened Christian must judge for himself. The Church, catching up with her more progressive members, begins to demand the application of Christian ethics to regions once left to the control of automatic law, like buying goods and investing money. A pioneer excitement attaches to the penetration of these regions. And very soon, in reaction from the difficulties encountered there, comes the obvious suggestion, since the present order is so involved in wrong that to Christianize it is at best a task of infinite subtlety and delicacy, and at worst may prove impossible,—why not leave it altogether? From the earliest Christian days, ardent souls have yearned for a complete renunciation of the world. Is not the way out a new Franciscanism, which shall lure men to throw away all that others hold precious in a divine madness, and to abandon themselves recklessly to love?

Introduction

If it could be done! But how can it? The entire repudiation of worldly goods, the severance from earthly ties, so familiar to exalted and eager souls in the Middle Ages,— are we self-deceived in finding it harder to compass now than then? Short of a monastery or a desert, neither of which was Francis's idea or the idea of Jesus, one cannot renounce the world. It creeps into the tissue of our simplest clothing, it lurks in our shelters, it penetrates our food. And ought one to try to renounce it? Apart from the basic impossibility of the thing, apart from one's weakness, two obstacles stand in the way.

The first is our honest modern disbelief in asceticism. We no longer feel the world to be a peril or an evil, we find in it the Sacrament of God's Presence, and the motive driving men to withdraw from it is no longer plain. Perhaps we moderns are making a mistake here. It is conceivable that a reaction may come, and an ascetic revival, perhaps reaching us from the East, may be in order. But, the second obstacle is more surely honorable, for it is found in the very growth of social feeling. Twentieth-century minds cannot sympathize unreservedly with St. Francis flinging his garments in his father's face; they cannot help thinking of the father! The tender duties, that held Tolstoy to the end from his heart's desire, hold us all. This is not weakness. It is the growth of democracy, making us indifferent to saving ourselves by ourselves, inhibiting us from claiming perfection at the cost of hurt to others. We are all involved together, and to break loose, leaving our dear ones in the net, is no way to follow Love. That old selfish way, which ended in serenely creating a spiritual aristocracy, was natural to aristocratic ages, but it is now alien to our best instincts. We no longer find our solution in a segregated Christianity; for we have learned to pray, Thy Kingdom come on earth. Not that we Christians are wholly thrown back by any means on self-indulgence and conformity. It is our business to obey the Church, to apply her now specific commands: We are to profit by exploitation as little as we possibly can; to simplify our lives to the farthest feasible degree; to practise detachment, and consecration, in the interior life of the soul. But we must tread warily lest we tread on hearts; and in seeking the far vision we may not neglect the primary tendernesses which also are of God.

But just as the old line of escape from sin grows more obscure, new lines are opening. The day is to the common life, the common effort. What we are not able to do as individuals, we may do all together, or through group-action. To use a homely simile, many Christians find themselves caught on the branches of a great tree, the tree of privilege. They do not quite know how to climb down, but they have the axe of the law in their hands, and they can apply themselves to sawing off the branch they sit on. No less than this, probably, is demanded of them by their religion, and it is consoling to reflect that, though a tumble may hurt, the ground is a good place after all.

Suppose all Church members brought their allegiance in great groups to movements which aim at restoring land and other wealth on equal terms to all men, and at placing the control of production in part at least in the hands of the producers. It is a startling hypothesis, but it is not inconceivable. Already it is happening in a measure. The Kingdom of God cometh not with observation, and it will never be possible to estimate the direct share of Christian idealism in recent progress toward industrial democracy. But the hour has come to increase that share dramatically and visibly. The sight of Christendom has surely braced and sobered Christian thought. If we are to avoid such catastrophe as has fallen on our neighbors, we must immediately apply Christianity to life, we must try to restore justice in America at the roots of things. Our prosperity, won at such fearful cost to other nations, gives us such chance at expiation and at social experiment as we have never had before; and the distinctive contribution of religion to the modern crisis is to encourage its more prosperous disciples to ally themselves with the tendencies which will impoverish them and handicap their power. In spite of all discouraging facts, which the following papers clearly recognize, the Church is beginning to say brave words. It is for her members to seal them with brave deeds.

IV

If in these papers the note of criticism sounds harsh at times, let it not be the last to linger on the ear. Not for a moment can a child of the Church forget the faithfulness of the "Mighty Mother" in fulfilling her primary duty. That duty is to keep open the channel between the temporal and the Eternal, through sacraments, through the Word of God, through all those disciplines of the interior life sanctified by the experience of questing generations. Unnumbered souls fed at her Altars day by day by the Bread of Pilgrims, will attest that she is true to her charge. To ignore this secret sacred work, to throw it into the background while impatient stress is put wholly on Church responsibility for solving social problems, would be to join the forces of Anti-Christ. The enduring task and glory of the Church is to foster in man the consciousness of God and to help him to union with his Maker.

But salvation, which is health and wholeness, can be won by no man alone. Social action becomes the swift correlative of spiritual vision. The regenerate man is the citizen of that Kingdom of Justice which is the Kingdom of God. And as perpetual intercession rises in the words of the Lord's own prayer, for the coming of this kingdom on earth, our social passion becomes, as it were, incorporated with our very conception of God. For He whom we adore is God on the Rood of the world. It is the God involved in the process of time, in the flux of mortal history: the God defeated, crucified, Whom we, by His mysterious will must aid if He is to come to His own. Our hands, alas, have nailed Him to that cross; without our help He cannot, because He will not, descend from it; and to aid Him we must climb to His side. Always men try to evade, to find ways of consecrating life without sacrificing it. And always, in measure as they are near to Christ, they fail. By the cross "the world is crucified unto me, and I unto the world." If the phrase is to regain a lost reality, it must be translated into social terms. The "world" to which it refers, to which it bids us be crucified, must be the world of the banker, of the merchant; of the solid business men who are the support of parishes; of the ladies from the leisure class who carry on the work of the Church. Love, seeking to save, saving if need be by dying, must be the inward law, expressed in outward life, related to actual present conditions, of every soul in-oned with Christ in the work of world-redemption.

In proportion as the Church can show how such sacrificial love can manifest itself through the present industrial and political situation, she will furnish the moral and spiritual leadership for the lack of which modern radicalism despises her, and the absence of which in that very radicalism makes the radical movement, to a Christian, superficial and suspect.

THE ALLEGED FAILURE OF THE CHURCH TO MEET THE SOCIAL EMERGENCY[1]

(A PAPER READ AT THE CHURCH CONGRESS HELD IN NORFOLK, VA., MAY, 1916)

I

BE it said at the outset that the title of this paper is not of my choosing. I should have left out the word "alleged."

The failure of the Church seems patent to-day when one looks at the spectacle of the world. Over in Europe, they say, many crosses have been spared in the general devastation,—so strangely spared that whispers of miracle pass about. On the roads over which move grim processions marching to kill, sad processions retreating to suffer, the Christ looks down:

[1] Reprinted from *The Yale Review*, January, 1917.

The Church and the Hour

"His sad face on the Cross sees only this,
After the passion of two thousand years."

Sometimes the figure stands unscathed when the Church that sheltered it is a ruin. Here is such a picture:

"All that is left of the building is a few white arches. Leaning forward from what remains of the wall at one end is a pale Figure, with arms widely extended, a wreath of thorns on its head. Shells have smashed away from it the wooden cross to which the arms were nailed; they seem now opened wide in a gesture of entreaty. . . . One must admit the ironic contrast of a Christ unscathed in a shattered Church. The persistence of the Figure, the dissolution of the fabric! The Church is man's interpretation of Christianity: but the Church has disappeared in this war of Christians; the Christ remains."

So the onlooker, expressing a widely spread attitude. And what can those say to whom the Church is infinitely more than "man's interpretation of Christianity"? To them also, are not these Calvaries looking down on battle-fields a tragic symbol, not of war only but of the civilized world?

If these years teach anything new, it is that civilization *per se* has little especially admirable about it. Civilization is no end in itself, as men have assumed it to be; it is merely an instrument, to be turned to use either by the forces of evil or by the forces of good. Have the forces of good, led by the churches, yet captured it? The answer, No, rises confused but unmistakable; the war has brought into terrible relief the persistent fact, that the Church, divided, hesitant, backward, has apparently no contribution to make, as an official body, either toward the healing of the nations or toward the healing of social disorders.

In Europe, churches are in use as observation-posts; they serve as shelter to the wounded or the homeless; from time to time the One Sacrifice is pleaded piteously from their ruined altars. But in collective effort to prevent the horror or to end it, the Church has been helpless. In effort to de-Paganize industrial and social life, is she not equally helpless the world over? Despite the frequent facile assumption that Christianity has undergone a great social revival, the reply must be, Yes. Religion has consoled the bereaved, it has strengthened the dying, it has established vast works of philanthropy; but for any statesmanlike attempt to evolve justice between nations or classes by the application of the law of Christ, men have looked to it in vain.

Last December I saw a strange Christmas tree. It was in the home of a German friend, whose tree is usually lovely with the radiant symbols of the Christ-Child. This year, no star, no angel, graced the summit; there was no manger at the base, with adoring shepherds and sweet Mother-Maid. The traditional eagle of Odin spread his wings on the topmost twig, and the snake, whom our Northern forefathers saw at the roots of the world-tree Ygdrasil, coiled with red tongue poisonously stuck out, high among the branches. "The tree has always belonged to the snake; it was a mistake to suppose that the Christ-Child had killed him," said my friend bitterly.

No, let us not say "alleged." "Alleged" has a defiant note. It calls for an apologia, a rebuttal. But in this year of grace,—and sin—excuse is no attitude for the Church or her children. Corporate penitence behooves us rather. We belong on our knees confessing our wrong-doing, not on our feet defending ourselves.

II

The normal tissue of our national life has obviously not been woven by Christianity. Our economic and industrial order is the natural outgrowth of forces with which religion has had nothing whatever to do. Many of these forces are to-day generally regarded as obsolescent; and the indictment against the Church is that she does nothing in particular to hasten their disappearance.

It is an indictment hard to disprove, but not particularly hard to explain. Though Christians be penitent, they must also regard the situation with common sense, and recognize the fallacy that mingles with truth in radical attacks on the Church.

These attacks habitually speak of the Church as if she were a separate body, responsible for converting State and society. The truth is more subtle. The Church is not a separate body, it is an interpenetrating force. The baptized individuals who compose it are to a large degree the same who compose State and society, and the Church in her corporate action can never take a stand which her members in their other capacities would repudiate.

Suppose five people constitute the Church in a certain village. Henry is a mill-owner, Patrick a hand in his factory, Mary is Patrick's wife, John a clerk in the bank, Kate is John's daughter, married to a stockholder in Henry's mill. Problem: to gain from these people a corporate mind concerning the wage-scale in that mill. One other person must be added: Peter, the parson. Now there is much to be said in favor of an old custom by which the Church in that community meant just Peter and nobody else. That custom, however, is obsolete among us; and regret is less, because it was partly based on the assumption that Peter was a perfectly disinterested person as well as a specialist in morals. Unfortunately, Peter's social relations are mainly with Henry and his family; moreover, he derives his subsistence from Henry. I believe this fact does not always prejudice him, but it does make his situation difficult, especially as he uses most of his salary to educate some heathen in the far Black Country.

And the community expects the Church to solve the labor-problem!

Now of course a large share of responsibility, though not the whole, does devolve on Peter. The clergy must guide us. But the point is that the business of the Church, as represented by Peter and his flock, is not to work from outside on a recalcitrant world, but to accomplish the far more difficult task of converting itself,—a task so difficult that it would never be accomplished save by the aid of supernatural grace.

In this interpenetration of Church and world, the reason is found for that lagging timidity which keeps the Church as an institution in the rear rather than in the van of social progress. We shall never again see a Church dictating terms to the secular world, unless we return to the discarded method of trusting her decisions to a hierarchy instead of to the

The Church and the Hour

whole body of the faithful; and that was not a particularly successful method, for ever since the Gift of Constantine, clergy as well as laity have remained a part of the very order which they would transform. It would therefore seem hopeless to expect from the Church a standard immeasurably ahead of her time. The positions she takes can hardly be quite out of reach of the common mind, for the common mind has dictated them.

How disparate the elements are which compose this mind is evident as soon as any common action is sought. To prove the slow growth of the social sense it is only necessary to try praying together without falling back on liturgies. Union in prayer must surely precede union in action; but in any praying group concerned with the social situation, each member will try to press his own specific, and the formulæ may tend ludicrously to neutralize each other. Here is a petition that the socialist party may gain votes, here one for the suppression of socialism; here pleads a suffragist, here an anti. And preparedness! What a Babel of voices, all perfectly good Christian voices, has been buzzing of late around the Throne! That they all may be One, prayed Our Blessed Lord; but He never meant one in opinion.

III

Yet when the very utmost is allowed for contradictions in Christian thought, when inclusiveness is pushed to the limit, it will be found that there is a region below opinion, deeper than dissent. In certain basic social principles unity must obtain, otherwise the Church must simply cease to be. These principles are so plain that, once stated, Christians have no option. They are indissolubly related to the peculiar treasures which the Church exists to guard. Who, nurtured on the Sacrament of Brotherhood, can stay contented with our present social order when once eyes have been opened? Who can really read the Gospels and fail to find them a disturbing force? In the intimacies of Christian experience, in the very sanctuary of faith, men seeking to learn the mind of Christ discover over and over the revolutionary nature of true discipleship:

"Where'er His chariot takes its way
The gates of death let in the day."

This has always been the case. However conservative the Church has been in her corporate and official capacity, radicals in all ages have been nursed at her breasts. But it is more the case to-day than at any previous time since the first century; for modern Christendom has awakened with a start of recognition to the historic purpose of her Master,—the establishment of the Kingdom of God on earth. This means the moralizing of life in its ultimate practical relations. Through the roar of battle and of factory, the Master's summoning Voice sounds stern.

Moreover, while the Church has lagged behind, great lay movements of unrest and of reconstruction have arisen and clamor for allegiance. She has not originated these movements; we must accept the fact that her official spirit cannot be adventurous. But when other adventurers have blazed the trail, she will be eternally disgraced if she does not follow.

Discrimination is necessary. There are

phases in these movements on which she can have no convictions. To measures like suffrage or anti-suffrage, to theories like socialism or syndicalism or single-tax, the Church cannot commit herself, though her members will naturally use their Christian ideals as a touchstone for all such propositions. There are other phases where her inaction would be a scandal and a crime. Perhaps the type of social reforms which Christianity must endorse, or perish, might be described by the phrase, "preliminaries to sanctification." It is an awkward phrase; but it obviously covers all measures aiming directly at the preservation of personality; it would apply to movements, legislative or private, demanding social sacrifice and self-control. It would include every statement in the admirable program of the Federation of Churches.[1]

Many points in this program deal with industrial conditions, and with these, sanctification may at first sight appear to have little to do. But a moment's thought shows that it has a great deal. The Church, like her Master, is in a way more concerned over the spiritual state of the prosperous than over

[1] See p. 7 ff.

that of the poor, and her anxiety about social justice springs largely from the fact that so long as the rich and fortunate countenance unbrotherly things, sanctification is impossible for them. It may be good for the soul of Patrick to subsist on a starvation wage, but it is very bad for the soul of Henry the mill-owner to pay him that wage. It is spiritual suicide for the possessors of privileges to rest, until such privileges become the common lot. This truth is what the Church should hold relentlessly before men's eyes; it is what makes indifference to social readjustments impossible to her shepherding love.

One does not see the sanctified man, for instance, defending his property rights with passion. A proposal has been made in a report of the Industrial Relations Commission that private bequests be limited to a million dollars. This is a reasonable and moderate proposal. It does not attack private property, but merely limits it at a point far above what most people reach, and no Christian mind would surely stoop to the meanness of claiming that it would unduly lessen incentive. It would deliver many men from fearful temptations,—a result for which we are told to pray. Incidentally, non-Christian moralists are pleading for self-limitation in wealth as the next step in the higher ethics. Now in view of Christ's persistent feeling that it is dangerous to be rich,—a feeling that no subtle exegesis has ever succeeded in explaining away,—one might have expected to see His disciples, His Church, eagerly welcome the plan and press it with enthusiasm. Did one see this spectacle? One did not.

Again, no Christian can remain indifferent or non-partisan toward movements for the protection of the weak. If the Church really possessed that homely family sense so touchingly expressed in the collect for Good Friday, most social problems would be solved. It may be materialistic to object to external poverty and sordidness; but no one has a right to say so unless he is prepared to welcome such conditions for his own relatives. It may be superficial to look to legislation as a cure for social evils; but the people who think so must be prepared with other cures. They must not be permitted to fall back on charity, whether "scrimped and iced" or warm and efficient; that solution is far outgrown. Neither may they dismiss the subject with the sententious remark that the one thing necessary is a change of heart. Necessary? Certainly! Change of heart is the beginning, it is not the end. Changed hearts all around, by hundreds and by thousands, are trying to express their conversion in social action. Has the Church no guidance to give to hearts when they have been changed?

If such matters as those indicated have nothing to do with the Church, then the Church has nothing to do with righteousness. The hour has come for Christian thought to give definite sanction to the new social ethic that has been developing for the last half century. The check by common will on private greed, the care for public health, the protection of childhood and manhood, the securing of fair leisure from the monotonies of modern labor, form a program hardly to be called radical any longer. It is accredited by all the progressive forces of the community, it forms the background of respectable modern thinking. But it has not yet emerged into respectable doing. That is another matter;

involving effort and sacrifice. Is not this just where the Church might come in? She has missed the chance at initiative; the chance of performance remains with her.

Let us not for a moment tolerate the contemptuous excuse for her too frequent silence, proffered by the radicals,—that her resources come from the sinners. Perhaps there are no sinners; perhaps there are only good men, blind. But assuredly they are very blind. Is the Church habitually giving them help to see? Is Church membership a guarantee that in time of stress a man will act on a higher level than mere business honor? A group of manufacturers fights organized labor, only to acknowledge, when the strike is won, that a rise was well warranted by the profits. Confronted by this disgraceful sight, does any one think to enquire how many of these employers were Church-members?

The standards of the Church in this matter of social morality should be no niggling minimum. They should be bold and explicit. She should make every Christian woman ashamed of herself so long as she neglects to secure a cleaner conscience by buying Consumer's League goods. She should make every Christian man ashamed of himself, so long as he is unable or unwilling to pay a living wage to his least employee. She should bid dividend holders be prepared to suffer rather than to profit by the exploitation of the laborer. Shrunken dividends can cause much distress, but as a class, by and large, the dividend holders are better off than the wage-earners. Poorest first is Christian law. Just wages should be the first consideration, reasonable dividends the second, personal profits for the directors the last. To reverse the order is usual nowadays; but it is Pagan.

And is it too much to hope that where a moral issue is plain, the Church might even occasionally get a little ahead of the community conscience, instead of always lagging a little in the rear?

Concerning that matter of dividends, for example. There is a growing healthy touchiness everywhere about the sources of wealth. In England feeble protests even arise,—oh, the shame of it!—against bishops' holding shares in breweries. As social imagination quickens, it becomes harder to accept income without knowing what that income connotes. Some radicals, to be sure, do not believe in the principles of interest at all; and it does no harm to dream of a day when the complex system involving it will be replaced by a more direct relation between services and rewards, class distinctions vanishing in consequence. But in the meantime many people must continue to live on the proceeds from stocks and bonds; and it is reasonable to wish to be sure that the money has not been gathered at the cost of cruelty or graft.

To profit by conditions which leave one uneasy is demoralizing and dangerous. A quarter century ago, much uneasiness concentrated itself among women upon the morale of buying; to meet it arose the Consumers' League. To-day the Christian stockholders of the United States begin to demand a White List of investments. Such a list if heeded would introduce a new principle into investing, quite apart from the size or security of the dividend. It would be a terrible nuisance. It would call for real sacrifice. Dozens of cogent reasons prove it impossible. In famous words, I am not concerned with the possibility of it,—only with the necessity. Perhaps it cannot be done, but that is a serious conclusion to reach. For the only Christian alternative to moralizing the present order is to abolish it, and if the Church cannot accomplish the first alternative, she must address herself with all speed to the second—which spells revolution.

Obviously, the Church is not herself competent to draw up such a white list of investments. Only trained experts could carry through so delicate, so intensely difficult a task. But I submit that it is for her to crystallize and encourage the new demand in the name of the torn consciences of her children. Through pulpits, forums, Sunday-schools, guilds, conferences, she can hold it clear before the public eye. Organized groups of Christian stockholders, studying the problem, feeling their way toward concerted action, rise before the fancy. And why could not the Church appoint her own commission of experts? She raises great funds: funds for philanthropy, for missions, for the relief of her aged clergy. Why not a fund to render her more fortunate children secure that their income is not drawn from Sunday labor, child-labor, or any unfair exploitation of the workers? The mere existence of such a commission would give her new status among reformers and among those alienated from her. It would serve as a visible witness that organized Christianity was in earnest. It would moreover tend automatically to establish the standard it approved, for it would offer strong moral support to the many in the younger generation of employers and financiers whose hearts are set on the improvement of industrial conditions.

IV

Schemes are easy to propose. This one calls for limitless wisdom, intelligence, tact, and pluck. And all the while the smooth voices of the world proclaim the *status quo* so pleasant,—and insinuate so plausibly that questions of this sort are irrelevant to religion!

The world has always taken the same line. The Church used to solve the problem of standards more easily in some ways than she can now. Formerly as always she worked in two fashions,—by permeating the ideals of society, and by contradicting them. A level of conduct slightly higher than if there had been no Church at all was accepted without qualms for the majority; but severe Counsels of Perfection shone aloft, luring the valiant to follow. And follow they did in throngs,—Regulars, Third Orders, Confraternities,—the chivalry of Christ, aiming at literal obedience to Him, vowed to conduct that contradicted at vital points the standards around them. We are all for permeation nowadays, and perhaps,—though the claim is timid,—religion really permeates a little more than it did. But there would be difficulty in reasserting the counsels. Mixing up mediocrity with democracy in our usual way, we have grown insensibly to such feeling for the common man that we distrust demands which he is not likely to approve. Also, the asceticism which held that holiness must repudiate life has yielded to enthusiasm for life in its fullness. These instincts are in their way creditable enough; but they result in a slackening of Christian ethics. As the Bishop of Oxford said years ago, religion suffers from diffusion at the cost of intensity.

What accredited type of piety did the United States inherit from the last century? Suave-mannered, pleasant-voiced; endangering nothing in particular, an ornament to the Sunday pews; devoted to good causes in proportion to their remoteness, intent on promoting safe philanthropies and foreign missions, but, so far as home affairs are concerned, ignorant alike of the ardors of the mystic and the heroisms of the reformer. A queer type of Christianity if one thinks of it,—cheerfully assuming that what is innocently agreeable is religious. Agonies of the social conscience deprecated in the name of spirituality, agonies of the inward life yet more deprecated in the name of sanity. No agonies at all, if you please: careless dependence rather than on an affectionate God, confusedly mixed with a sentimental love of scenery. Parents more concerned with hygiene than with salvation for their offspring; sacrifice relegated to the foreign field, or to underpaid social workers. A domestic religion, mid-Victorian in effect, calculated to make life pleasant in the family circle,—but curiously at ease in Zion.

That was about what Christianity meant in many a home three years ago.

Then came the war, with its appeal for devotion to the uttermost; and the peoples of Europe responded with a sort of sacred joy. They obey the call of governments to destroy fellow-men at any personal cost in the name of patriotism; and their readiness puts to shame the failure of the Church to enlist them for the protection of manhood, in the holier Name of Christ.

The excuse for the contrast is of course that men will always be ready to defend ancient sanctities; it requires imagination as well as courage to break new ways for Love to enter. Yet how tempting to picture a new crusade, that should win for Christ the whole sphere of social and industrial relations! Here is the Adventure of the waiting world; and the Church should call men to it with a trumpet.

In the great strange years to come, will she call them; will she guide them? On the answer lies the salvation of civilized life. Battle-smoke overhangs those years: it drifts across the narrow seas, so blinding that we in America cannot discern our future. But this is sure, that after the war old evils will be fiercer than ever, while aspirations toward righteousness also will be fired with a new intensity. Realities become masked with the advance of civilization. Many masks have fallen now, many conventions are destroyed. The social order is seen stark naked: it is not a lovely sight. In passing, one may notice that the convulsion which has stripped humanity, was not caused by the radical forces once so dreaded, but, one is almost tempted to say, by the Devil himself, masquerading as gentleman, patriot, and diplomatist. In the hideous glare of the firing, it is possible to see Mars and Mammon, twin supporters of the old Capitalistic order, rushing on their own destruction.

This is the hour of opportunity; this is the hour of the Church. In the last fifty years she has accomplished a great preparation, by her rediscovery of the purpose of Jesus. Few and hesitant, however, have been her attempts to realize that purpose, to strive boldly, through profound labors of readjustment and reconstruction, to establish the Kingdom of God, the kingdom of love, on earth. Perhaps one cause of her semi-paralysis has been her failure to recognize that the central incident in the process of establishing the kingdom must always be a Cross.

If civilization, with its science, its culture, its thousand graces of heart and mind, is not to be abandoned to the powers of evil, the revolutionary principle of love must be accepted as the practical basis for all human relations, industrial and national.

V

But, for the Christian, what a tremendous IF!

The central question will not down: Has religion anything to do with civilization? Perhaps the age is sweeping to catastrophic end,—and in that case the true aim of the Christian is not to transform the social order, but to transcend it. So thought the Early Church: her Christianity was largely uninterested in secular affairs, and her disciples, adopting an *ad interim* policy toward the evil world from which they had been saved, awaited, patient, humble, the coming of the

Son of Man. "Even so, come, Lord Jesus!" That last prayer of the Scripture canon is still the final prayer on Christian lips; and still the echo of the Lord's own question stings the heart: When the Son of Man cometh, shall He find faith on the earth?

Trust in progress has received a shock of late. But even before the war, a strong current in the religious world was considering it an illusion, and setting toward those Apocalyptic hopes always accompanied with other-worldly fatalism. Books like Hugh Benson's *Lord of the World*, and the Russian Solovyof's brilliant *War Progress and the End of History*, expressed the curious idea that the modern humanitarian movement, if it were not Anti-Christ himself, was at least a preparation for Anti-Christ; talk concerning the Second Advent was revived in unexpected quarters, and mysticism, with its stress on the interior life as the only matter of importance, entered its ancient claim in new and lovely forms.

Perhaps few people hold explicitly the belief in an apocalyptic as opposed to a social type of Christianity. But this is the extreme of an instinctive reaction. While social Christianity, weak and young, reaches out pleading arms for help, suspicion of it has set in. Growing opposition threatens between two Christian schools, one humanitarian, philanthropic, even socialistic, stressing the establishment of the Kingdom of God on earth; the other mystic, individualistic, intent exclusively on the development of spiritual faculty, on the release of eternity in Time. This last school, I suppose, would not oppose temporal works of mercy when they clamored to be done; but it would take slight interest in attacking those hidden wrongs basic to the present social order. No white list of investments needed for its followers!

Something in most of us shares the distaste for social Christianity. And no wonder. Cant about social service fills the air. The complacent young make it an excuse for the neglect of penitence and devotion. The hungry sheep leave Church, swollen less often with theological wind than in Milton's day, but with sociological chaff, which is no more nourishing. Earnest people go to Church very wistful, and what they crave from Christian preaching is not instruction about reforms. They want release for the frozen springs of will and feeling, power imparted to open the soul to the inflowing Grace of God. Too often, the modern pulpit evades their need. Too often, the modern Church seems like a great machine for the cheery promotion of social welfare, and it is natural enough if the charge is made that social service, and care for social justice, is simply that clever old enemy materialism, invading the sanctities in new disguise.

Personally, I believe that there is one way only of avoiding the menacing division between spiritual and social Christianity. I believe that the reproach of unspirituality, so often and so justly cast on social religion, is mainly due to the frequent divorce between social enthusiasm and Christian dogma; and that the special power of the Church to meet the social emergency depends on the presence within her of a large group to whom the two aspects of her heritage are alike precious and essential, and who draw their social radicalism from the Catholic faith in its wholeness.

The great movement of social reform and revolution will go on, as it began, quite independently of Christian people. But if the Christian will has a distinctive contribution to make, such a contribution must spring from the distinctive Christian convictions. Reform, revolution, have for the Christian one supreme aim,—the general release of human power, so that men may more truly know God and enjoy Him forever. This is the end of all our "preliminaries to sanctification." Unless a man know within himself this supreme aim, how can he rightly further it for others? And what is the Catholic faith, except the ultimate means for attaining the knowledge of God verified by the Christian experience of the ages?

This attitude is unpopular, and it is currently assumed that revolt from dogma and zeal for social reform are mysteriously connected. Significant books illustrate this thesis; brilliant men defend it. It is a plausible thesis, for the alliance is natural and common. All instincts of revolt sympathize while they are immature, and reaction against the accredited in religion and in society is likely to make a simultaneous appeal to the mind. Yet treacherous accidents of time or origin can bring into temporary alliance movements either unrelated or opposed. Communism, for instance, to many among its disciples and its critics alike, implies hostility to marriage. But the basis of sex relations and property relations is quite diverse, and there is no earthly reason why community in goods should imply community in wives. Nor is there any reason either earthly or heavenly, why disbelief in the Virgin-Birth or the Trinity should predispose a man to oppose vested interests or sweatshops.

The modern churches are full of people who find dogma a clog to the free spirit, and who concern themselves with it as little as may be. Let them stay, and work for righteousness. But let them recognize the value of the other school, who apprehend Christianity less as ethical program than as spiritual power, and whose firm faith in Catholic doctrine is the well-spring of revolutionary conviction. There is intimate union, known to many who shrink from speaking of these arcana, between the Catholic faith at its fullest and social radicalism at its boldest. Strength comes to these, not from such generalized religious ideals as can be shared by Buddhist or Jew, but from the definite Gospel as interpreted by the historic Church. They leave the religion of Humanity to those without the churches, for they know a better thing,—the religion of Christ.

Religious fervor, as the past proves, is attended by a vicious danger of spiritual egotism, unless it lead to social action. But plain Christians generally know to-day, as they have always known, that for them social action is in the long run unmotived and perilous unless it draw from deep wells of religious faith.

VI

And if any say, as they will, that dogma is a dead thing, irrelevant to these reflections and to the love of God, let them remember that most Christian doctrines are simply experience taken at white heat and crystallized. Because experience is concerned with relationships, the richest social implications may be drawn from all the great theological concepts of the Church. For instance: to casual surface thinking, nothing seems more remote from daily life or more repellent than the more recondite phases of the doctrine of the Atonement. Yet nowhere can heroism be more truly quickened, nowhere can modern ethic be more severely rebuked, than in contemplating the amazing depths of love which the Church stumblingly tries to describe in that doctrine. Jealousy for the welfare of one's children is a central point in this ethic of ours: to protect them is a cardinal duty, and a far stronger deterrent from radical change than personal ambition or fear; many and many a man would risk all for himself who will risk nothing for his child. Yet the Beloved Son, begotten before all worlds, is sent forth by the Father to suffer even unto death for the world's salvation; thus are our timidities put to shame; and the worshiper, contemplating the Atonement from the point of view not of man but of the Fount of Godhead, learns readiness to sacrifice not only himself, which is easy, but his children, which is hard.

Only by cherishing the tremendous impetus to bold social action to be found in the mystical depths of dogma can the modern social movement be rescued from the half-deserved reproach of putting the body above the soul, and losing sight of the eternal in the things of time. And many believe that only by drawing from this source can the movement gain permanent force to withstand the fierce passions of the lower nature, and to create the new era in which the impossible paradox shall be realized, righteousness and peace kissing each other, and mercy and truth meeting as lovers at last.

And in proportion as we draw from such source of strength, perhaps the question concerning the reality of human progress will cease so actively to distress us,—though we may be no more able to give a categorical answer to it than our Master was. It is clear that in the mind of Jesus, as in history, two principles were recognized about the Coming of the Kingdom: growth and catastrophe. When His Church loses thought of catastrophe, and devotes herself comfortably —and half-heartedly—to furthering growth, omens of future judgment are likely to gather, as they are gathering now. We shall do well if, obeying Christ's indubitable teachings, we join to our steadfast efforts to promote the cause of the Kingdom on earth, the awestruck readiness for sudden judgment. Of that day and that hour knoweth no man, and the kingdom cometh not with observation; but it is sure to come. And we are to remember that in the New Testament judgment is the goal of hope, the beginning and not the end; since it ushers in that millennium which is no heavenly mirage, but the Christian Utopia, the destined heritage of fleshly men.

Meantime let us not soothe our slothful wills because Our Lord delayeth His Coming. Nothing is clearer than that Christ condemns inactivity. We must increase our talents, we must tend our lamps, we must work in the vineyard as if the harvest time were sure. To the prayer, *Thy Kingdom come on earth*, which carries with it so certain a promise of fulfilment, must be joined that other last prayer without which the heart would fail indeed: *Even so come, Lord Jesus*. It is the supreme test of faith to live in uncertainty, and to that test our age is called. This means that in a peculiar sense, inward and mystic as well as practical, it must embrace the heroic aspects of the Cross.

The world has never been so conscious of Christ as in these days of horror. Cartoons show Him everywhere. The hand of the dead soldier rests on His wounded Feet; the sorrowing wife feels His consoling Presence. Kaiser and King turn their backs on Him or pierce Him with the bayonet. To His gray figure on the Cross, touched with dawn in the mists that rise from the profounds of mountain chasms, climb bowed processions of phantom mourners, chanting in all the tongues of the warring nations to Him Who is their Peace. Meantime, those actual Calvaries that stand so grave and still, watching the battle-fields, bring a message of hope rather than despair. Though the walls of the Church seem shattered, and though no rest be found for the seeking soul in its ruins, it cannot perish so long as Christ abides. For His presence creates it, and that presence, manifest on its Altars, shall never leave the world He died to save.

THE CHURCH'S OPPORTUNITY

The Christian Church, especially in Anglo-Saxon countries, is awakening to an extraordinary paradox in its position. This is not a new paradox; but never before was it so marked as in our day. It relates to the social quality of Church membership. The disinherited and the humble were the first to profess the faith, and the formulæ of that faith are theirs. The prosperous are those who now profess it, and the formulæ are strange upon their lips.

At the time of the first Christmas, the poor, the slaves, the oppressed, were craving a Deliverer, throughout that Roman Empire on whose upper circles "disgust and secret longing" had fallen. The sense of sin, growing curiously deep just then, blended with a confused resentment against injustice at the roots of things; the quickened personal life shared by the proletariat with the rest of the world, hungered for some aid to self-respect. How fully Christianity met these needs—Christianity, with its story of a Carpenter, despised and rejected, executed as an agitator, victor over death, Saviour from sins, who washed men in His blood and made them kings and priests before God! The new hope was born among workingmen. Secretly, swiftly, it spread through the Roman underworld, though an occasional "intellectual" as we might now say, rose to leadership in the movement. It swept through Asia Minor westward to the center of empire, thence out to farthest barbarian bounds. Many educated and prosperous people were before long touched by the rapture which so strangely blotted out worldly distinctions; yet in the main the faith percolated up from below, bearing the clear stamp of a proletarian religion. God had put down the mighty and exalted the humble. He had filled the hungry, while the rich were sent empty away. What though these marvels were achieved on the spiritual rather than the natural plane? All the more satisfying, all the more permanent. Blessed were the poor, the meek, the hungry for justice; the dispossessed and defeated lifted their brows to heaven to catch the light of a new morning, in which military valor, administrative power, intellectual acumen, slipped into shadow, and the radiance fell on the servile virtues which Paganism had scorned.

Of course the situation did not last long. Christianity was too rare a discovery to be left in the hearts of slaves. At first more or less a class-conscious movement, it was saved from being revolutionary also only by its apocalyptic hope, and by the instinct for non-resistance and obedience native to the classes through which it spread. But from the first it held the germs of a universal faith, and it slipped from the control of the proletariat as it had slipped from the control of the Jews. Before long, we find it approved by the authorities; and the Gift of Constantine, ("Ahi Costantin, di quanto mal fu matre!") united an institutional Catholicism firmly with the existing order. Fervent Christian missionaries now aimed at the conversion of princes, who, when converted, imposed the new religion wholesale on their realms, and brought the armies of their adversaries to baptism at the point of the sword.

These subject populations seem to have been genuinely Christianized after a fashion. We confront a mediæval Europe which in a sense deserves the name of Christendom; however childishly the religion be conceived, it is at least the common heritage. The feudal baron and his least of villeins are fed from the same altar and die with the same invocations on their lips. The faith, Catholic in more than name, encourages a spiritual democracy that goes far to mitigate the harshness of class-barriers, and to plant in race-consciousness, however obscurely, the seed of brotherhood. Through the middle ages, our paradox, however humorous, is innocent and unconscious. Cheerily the followers of the Prince of Peace go forth to war and live by the rule of might. Archbishop Turpin gives his Franks for penance an order to "fight their best"; Roland in one breath invokes St. Michael, and bids farewell to his sword, "the fair and holy,"— prototypes these of endless warrior prelates and most Christian, Catholic, and predatory nobles, on whose lips the Gospel maxims sound strange indeed. But men were simple then. The fighting had to be done, the authority to be maintained, and sunset years in a monastery might always atone for a vehement noon. Meanwhile, there were always the voiceless throngs of faithful, wistful people—villeins, vagrants, poor folk of the towns—to whom the vision of the city of peace, where the humble should reign, brought help and healing; men who cherished with passionate devotion their glorious secret: belief in the workman who had been cradled in a barn, had lived a houseless man, and who should be Judge and Overlord of all the great of the earth. "Our Prince Jesus poverty chose, and His apostles twelve; and aye the langer they lived the less goods they had." Honor poor men, "for in their likeness oft our Lord hath been known." So said old Langland patiently.

Do poor folk take like comfort to-day? One doubts it; for Christianity to all appearance, at least in Protestant countries, is certainly no longer in any general sense a proletarian religion. As we said at the outset it has largely passed into the hands of the privileged.

This is not to say in any sweeping absolute fashion that the Christian religion is obliterated among the lower classes. There is the Salvation Army, there are slum churches thronged at mass, there are many other honorable exceptions. Yet in the main it is difficult to deny that those who support and value the churches to-day are the comfortable middle classes, while those who first received the good tidings and spread it over the civilized world would surprise us very much if they appeared in the sanctuary. Fifty years and more ago, Matthew Arnold pointed out the divorce of the working people from religion as the most sinister sign of the times. He hoped to win them back by blotting out dogma in favor of ethics; but it is not the working class that has accepted his suave attenuations of the Gospel. To picture the congregation in a popular church, transformed into the sort of audience to be seen at a socialist rally or a strikers' meeting, is a startling flight of fancy. The hungry and the meek no longer sing the Magnificat. Respectable and relatively prosperous people fill the churches so far as they *are* filled; establish missions, guilds, and institutional centers for the class to which they owed their faith in the beginning; and worry seriously over the "lapsed masses."

Nor does one see any immediate prospect of change in the curious situation. The classes at the base of things suffer to-day under sorrowful pressure of industrial anxiety. Their members when gentle, have often too little vitality for church-going, and when spirited experience too sharp indignation at the heart-root to enjoy peaceful religious hope. General interest, among them, is largely transferred from another world to this one; a new religion, the dangerous religion of revolt, spreads like silent flame among the working classes. Eager in propaganda as the religion of Paul was once, it lures, it quickens, it wakes in dull eyes the light that Christianity no longer kindles. We may mourn as we will. We may analyze causes forever in the magazines. In sincere distress over souls that perish, we may multiply our missions; the situation will persist. The people who most loudly glorify submission and renunciation belong to the class least called on to practice these virtues; those who extol a homeless

Lord command fair homes where their children gather in peace around them, while the landless and homeless have wandered far from Him, and are seeking strange new guides.

What are we to learn from this situation?

No more extraordinary reversal was ever seen than the change, socially speaking, of the *personnel* of the Christian Church. There is little use in fighting the situation directly. There is less use in grieving over it. We shall do better to consider its good points, for it has them.

We may notice, for instance, that the well-to-do and respectable need religion quite as much as the proletariat—more, if we are to trust Jesus when He says that they are in peculiar spiritual peril. From this point of view, it is a cheering fact that to thousands of people in the prosperous classes religion is perfectly genuine. Loyalty to the Churches, does really foster in them the life of the soul, however hard working-class agitators find it to believe this. They break through into that "world subsisting within itself," which, as Eucken says, religion creates, and consciously submit their being to its transforming and saving power.

For over a century critics have been announcing that Christianity was at the point of death; but never was it more alive. We hardly need such proofs as a Men and Religion Forward Movement, a World's Student Christian Federation, a Conference on Faith and Order. Countless confraternities and guilds, Anglican orders revived, Roman orders dispersed on the Continent only to plant centers of influence in free Anglo-Saxondom, show the vitality inherent in the more rigid forms of faith; while a public that eagerly absorbs Eucken and draws enormous numbers of religious books from libraries, is surely awake to spiritual things. Emphases have changed. Ethics and sentiment interest more than dogma. That benevolence of which Christ said so little has become our central social virtue, replacing that joy in poverty and that spirit of renunciation for which He pleaded. None the less the cry arises, "Thou hast made us for Thyself, O Lord, and restless are our hearts until they rest in Thee."

So far so good; yet we all want to probe

further. Our paradox must hold a summons. For, to speak frank Christian language, if God has thus shaped Christian history, it is because He has thought it well so to do. The situation at any point of time—to believe this is the superb adventure of Christian faith—is that precise situation from which everyone involved may profit the most: it is that through which the Kingdom of God may advance more swiftly. The glory of every temptation, every difficulty, is the opportunity it presents.

What is the opportunity, what the summons, afforded in the dramatic transformation of Christianity from a religion of slaves to a religion of masters? The greatest we could ask. It is the chance to demonstrate, with a unique cogency, that Christianity is no mere natural product, but a supernatural power. We can rout for all time the economic determinist. We can prove, as Eucken says once more, that "reality has a depth beyond the natural man."

Early Christian history holds no such demonstration for the modern caviller. He points out that the new religion, with its emphasis on servile virtues, took facile root among a servile population. In the underworld of society a religion was bound to flourish which lent the grace of dignity and the light of spiritual romance to the qualities of non-resistance, unworldliness, and meekness, which the poor were in any case forced to practice, and exalted into honor the ancient badges of their shame. The early Christians sacrificed little: their religion was a natural product of their economic environment, as it remains to this day a natural consolation for the weak. Would you persuade us to see in it an influx of grace from Above, show it practiced by the strong!

Where do we so find it? Where perceive clear proof of the Christian ideal running counter to the psychology engendered by circumstance? One remembers interesting individuals, down the centuries: a Francis Bernardone, a Gordon, a Shaftesbury. They arrest thought, one admits. But look at life in the large! Christianity has been really operative only with those groups or classes to whom submission, obedience, are matters of necessity: Russian peasants, if you will, or Langland's poor folk, or women, before the days of the suffragettes. It has been easy enough for the crushed to honor meekness, for the suffering to console themselves by the secret faith that pain redeems the world, for people "terrified by fears, cast down by poverty" to praise poverty of spirit, and look forward to a Vision of Peace beyond the grave.

But let us see the powerful, for a change, abjuring their power; the rich, giving poverty more than lip-homage and patronage; the happy, deliberately choosing to suffer with the age-long hunger of the dispossessed, till they win the blessing of them that mourn. Show us a corporate Christianity which involves social sacrifice on a large scale. If you show that, you can bid us believe in anything, even in baptismal regeneration.

What is this? You point to the hold Christianity has on the prosperous classes? To our large congregations, our great contributions to missions and philanthropy, our solemn stress on "social service," our magnates of finance passing the contribution plate?— And here it is to be feared that the caviller pauses and shrugs. Amuse yourselves as you like, he says. Try as you will to add to the assets of one order of things, the earthly, the perquisites of another order, the heavenly; reserve your Christian principles for private consumption in the family circle, or treat them as an affair of the heart, sentimentally spiritual, unrelated to the way in which you make or spend your income. Evade as you choose the plain purport of your Master's teaching of brotherhood. The religion you profess may last your time, but it is as surely dying out as the plants in His old story withered from lack of soil. What we outsiders need in order to convince us that you Christians have indeed "broken through into reality" is to see those who can command luxury, choosing poverty so long as their brothers want; those who might rule men, industrially or politically, becoming true servants of the democracy. It is to find Christians voting in public matters steadily against their own class-interests, and in private life literally caring more to share than to own. This spectacle, we grant, would be an effective proof of a divine religion. But men are not likely to see it.

No? But what if they did?

Since the days of the martyrs, Christians have had no chance to bear witness so salient, so inviting, to the reality of their faith. The martyr is only the witness, though the connotations of pain that the word carries imply that honest witness-bearing has always involved cost. The test must be real. It was real in the Early Church, and people met it: nobles, of whom there was ever a fair sprinkling among believers, as well as slaves, to whom after all life was sweet. We may not have the martyr-stuff in us to-day. The very word has degenerated, till we speak, Heaven forgive us, of a martyr to rheumatism or to relatives! A martyr to us means a victim. Now comes the chance to redeem the word, to show that he is a hero. Reality endures. The nature of the witness it requires varies from age to age. These being the industrial ages, witness to truth will naturally be related to the industrial life; and it has strangely and quietly come to pass that Christian people are now chiefly drawn from the class which has industrial sacrifice within its power to make.

Obvious economic sacrifice on the part of Christians at large is the only sound means to silence the reiterated sneer of the materialistic radical who threatens our civilization. He is honestly convinced that no solid gain in justice or freedom has ever been carried through with the support of those who had anything to lose by it. Here is the slogan of the revolutionary syndicalist, here the insidious assurance through which he attracts the working people by thousands to his religion of revolt. He insists *ad nauseam* that every advance in popular freedom has been wrested with difficulty and violence by the oppressed from the oppressors. If you say that it is better to endure injustice than to seek justice by violence, he asks if you regret Runnymede and the Boston tea-party. If you remark sententiously that "nothing is ever achieved by violence," he retorts with some show of reason that little has ever been achieved otherwise. Plead with him to wait patiently till brotherly love shall accomplish its work, unaided by coarser powers, he will point a sinister finger at the workers, for instance, in the textile industries, remark that he is in a hurry, and challenge you to adduce specific instances on your side.

The Church and the Hour

And it must be confessed that he has you in a corner. You search history too often in vain to refute him. Instances of individual self-sacrifice are gloriously common: instances of corporate self-sacrifice are conspicuous by their absence. The most picturesque instance does not come from Christendom at all; it is the abnegation of the Japanese Samurai.

But that such instances have been rare in the past does not prove that they cannot occur in the future. Possibilities change. Democracy sinks in. It is bringing about a state in which the highest private ethics are impelled as never before to reproduce themselves in the collective ethics of the group. If its intuitions are genuine, they must engender, not merely neutrality but disinterested action. It must be proved, not by words but by deeds, that large masses of people are more affected by desire for the common good than by desire to protect their own interests.

Democracy of this type needs a spiritual instrument. Where can we look for such an instrument so naturally as to the Christian Church?

The Church can, to be sure, do little in her

corporate capacity. She is a spiritual, not an economic organism, and as such she can serve spiritual functions only. But the inspiration she supplies should guide her children in every province, and should to-day, above all, direct them toward social sacrifice. The chief hope of idealism in the present crisis is in the attitude and action of Christians from the prosperous classes. Will they hold to the solid, imperturbable tenets of their class, stubbornly defending a system alien to the spirit of their Master, even while professing in jejune generalizations to believe in His ideals? Or will they afford the most striking instance in history of a group-consciousness transcending lower forces, and acting directly from Above, counter to its own material advantage?

Should they so act, they would furnish an amazing spectacle indeed: a miracle, if you will. For class interest is a force so subtle, universal, irresistible, that to bid men defy it is like bidding the body defy gravitation, the lungs refuse to breathe.

Is it not thinkable that to the end of just this miracle, the striking transference of Christianity from the underworld to the world of comfort and prosperity, was determined in heavenly councils and brought about through slow historic process? Future Church historians may show with dramatic power how Christianity, at the crisis of its fate, had insensibly changed from the refuge of the proletariat to the home of the privileged in order that a triumphant demonstration of its divine nature might be afforded by the action of its followers, who in time of social revolution were chief agents in destroying all undue privilege by which they and their class could profit.

The virtues called for by Christianity are distinctly supernatural. They run athwart every instinct of unregenerate man; and to root them in the human soil, every advantage had to be taken. Even before the Christian era much had been done. To give the human animal the freedom of a higher than animal life, is a tremendous feat. At first the process was evident only at rare points and moments, as in maternal devotion, where the ego is promoted a little, only a very little way, out of its own self. When that potent help to the achievement of the high task, the Christian ideal, entered the world, it had first to sow its seed among the lower classes, because those classes could foster that seed best. Such conditions as Christianity found for its inception in Judæa, and encountered during its early progress in the Roman Empire, were a necessity for its survival. Renunciation, pity, meekness, had to commend themselves first to those who knew how to pity because they had suffered, to renounce because they had never possessed, who by force of their outward situation were prepared to find joy in persecution, peace in subjection, immortal hope in their lack of earthly good.

To their amazement they did find these things and found them precious. In the midst of their chains they became free, not by shaking off the chains, but by learning that in bondage is truest freedom. Disciplined through the ages in the mystic Christian joy, that joy became to them so intensely real that the wistful world of wealth and success, looking in their faces, reluctantly acknowledged a sweetness beyond all it had to give, and discovered itself an-hungered for the secret blessings of those beneath its feet. So even the prosperous and the happy learned to set their affections on things Above.

But the story could not end there. The Christian virtues may take long centuries to strike deep roots in lives not forced to them by circumstance; but the time comes when, if they are so rooted, they must blossom in triumphant and supernatural beauty. Otherwise our planet is a moral tragedy among the spheres.

To-day, after nineteen hundred years, we hope for a season of blossom. Because the majority of Christian folk are now born not to want but to reasonable comfort, they can, if they will, demonstrate practically that comfort is matter of indifference to them compared with love. In no fantastic asceticism but in sober modern fashion, let them renounce luxury in consumption, greed in acquisition, permitting their light to shine by allowing their motives to be known. Let them remember that there is that scattereth and yet increaseth. Above all, let them as members of the body politic and industrial quietly throw their adherence on the side of justice to the dispossessed, or, if this phrase does not appeal to them, of generosity to the weak.

Never have Christian people had a more dramatic opportunity. Will they embrace it? When the Son of Man cometh, shall He find faith on the earth?

TWO LETTERS TO "THE MASSES"[1]

The Masses is a radical weekly published in New York. It is clever, searching, clear-purposed, and bitterly anti-ecclesiastical. Its scathing cartoons well deserve attention from church-loving persons; as in the case of a drawing of prosperous clergy feasting at a table over which hangs a crucifix; below, a citation from the *Times* stating the cost of a clerical dinner to have been $5.00—or was it $10.00?—a plate; above, the caption, *Their Last Supper*.

But while the satire stings, some of it is grossly unfair, notably the contemptuous and ignorant attitude toward Christian dogma. Certain skits, imitating from afar the light irony of Anatole France, but unrelieved, to some minds at least, by Gallic delicacy or point, excited much criticism a year or two ago. These skits called forth a number of

[1] Reprinted from *The Masses*, Dec., 1915, and Feb., 1916.

letters, some protesting, some applauding, which the editors published in amusing juxtaposition. The quotations from the correspondence which follow are reprinted with the thought that they may indicate conditions in sincere radical minds which the Christian apologist must meet:

"Editors of *The Masses*,

"GENTLEMEN: You sent me an appeal for subscribers. Slowly and lazily I had just reached the point of getting you one when I received the 'Heavenly Dialogue' in your last month's issue. You will get no subscribers through me. I am not afraid of blasphemy, as I do not think the eternal verities are ever injured by it, and I like and approve sharp, clever attacks on all that is false and conventional in religion. But the smart and cheap vulgarity of that thing was too much for me. It is a pity.

"I have read few remarks about the war that struck home to me as did those by Max Eastman in the same number. . . .

"I wish *The Masses* could manage to avoid offensiveness with no sacrifice of its trenchant quality, and I think it could, perfectly well, if the editors chose to do so. . . .

"Fraternally and cordially,
"Vida D. Scudder."

A Western correspondent wrote:
"Keep hammering away at the failure of us who profess faith in the Lord Jesus Christ—we need it: we must never think we are following his ideals as closely as smug complacency suggests. But please do not serve up in your columns more of such articles as that to which I have referred, which alienate without benefiting—and which are in bad taste, I firmly believe."

The Masses retorted:
"Such a letter one can hardly answer at all, so remote is its viewpoint, and yet so warm its good-will. It is as if a being from some other planetary system should write in, asking why we assume that every heavy thing drops to the earth. We wonder how this being who lives under the Lord Jesus as an anthropomorphic God, ever wandered into the orbit of *The Masses*—and yet, now that he is there, we would like to hold his interest and

faith, for he evidently has a little faith in us.

"And perhaps there is some ground for it. We believe in Jesus. We believe that he lived and died laboring and fighting, in a noble atmosphere of disreputability, for the welfare and liberty of man. To us his memory is the memory of a hero, and perhaps a good deal of our indignation against the Church rises from that. We are indignant, not only because the Church is reactionary, but because the Church betrayed Jesus. The Church took Christ's name and then sold out to the ruling classes. The Church is Judas. And to us that little immaculate ikon that sits at the right hand of the image of God in Heaven is a part of the whole traitorous procedure. Whoever puts Jesus up there dodges Him down here—that has been our experience. Look into your mind and find out whether it *is* Jesus of Nazareth that you want to defend against satire, or a certain paste-and-water conception of Him which assuredly needs your defense."

It seemed worth while to comment a little further on this correspondence, so the following letter was written:

"To the Editor:

"With 'inward glee' if not with 'serious faith,' I read your Talk on Editorial Policy, wherein you print letters from candid friends, including myself, neutralizing each other. They are good fun.

"But I am moved to tell you something. It is apropos of the letter from California and your comment on it.

"What I want to tell you is that you have no cause for surprise at the sympathy of 'this being' for *The Masses*. He does not stand alone. It is high time for you to recognize that anti-Church radicals do not absorb radicalism any more than Church-members absorb Christianity. The old creeds are not dead, though impassioned believers in them are not often met, according to my experience, in 'cultured Boston' or its suburbs—or anywhere else. They exist, however, these believers—men and women who consider themselves, not merely with you, admirers of a dead martyrhero, but disciples of a Living Lord. Among these disciples a considerable number find the pungent and penetrating treatment of Churchianity and civilization in *The Masses* as welcome as flowers in May. They agree with you not all the time, but much of the time, and they give thanks for you and wish they were clever enough to do so too.

"For among those who know an interior union with the Living Christ (pardon the strange language) He is manifest more and more as the Christ of the Revolution.

"Of course, this vision of Him was long obscured. But it has never been lost. In the unpromising eighteenth century, William Blake defiantly proclaimed it:

'The vision of Christ which thou dost see
Is my vision's greatest enemy,
Both read the Bible day and night,
But thou readest black where I read white.

. . . .

Where'er His chariot took its way.
The gates of death let in the day'——

"So long as the Gospels are read aloud Sunday after Sunday in church, the vision can't be lost. It bides its time, it finds its own. It is most compelling to-day among those who believe,—they really do, I assure you,—that He who was executed by the combined forces of the religious, intellectual, and governing classes of His day, is to be the Judge of the human race.

"In gently assuming that no intelligent person who enjoys *The Masses* holds this extraordinary hope, Mr. Editor, you are provincial. Please socialize your mind! Please open imagination to the fact of which I inform you,—that there are plenty of people ready to stand shoulder to shoulder with you in the fight for a clean, just, democratic civilization, who get authentic inspiration from sources closed to you. And don't sneer at their sanctities; it isn't worth while. The most seeming-obsolete formula is likely to have a sacred heart beating in it. It has meant, at all events, something profound in human experience. Were I in Buddha-land, I should never make fun of even the most crude and popular forms of Buddha-worship. Were I among the Turks, I should say my prayers in the Mosques—always supposing (I am hazy on this point)—that they would admit a lady. *The Masses* lives in a country where a great deal of real Christianity survives—though I confess that appearances rather contradict the assertion. It wouldn't do you a bit of harm to show a little respect for it. For the amazing truth of the old Christian formulæ is plain to the experience of thousands, and great tides of Christian mysticism are rising to refresh the arid souls of our generation.

"I hardly expect you to be interested in all this. And nobody is trying to convert you. You are doing a lot of good just where you are, and we all have eternity, and possibly many lives ahead even on earth, in which to learn things we don't know. But as we muddle along together, it should be possible to believe people who tell us that they see a light we don't, and to accept them courteously as fellow-pilgrims toward the City of Equity.

"Fraternally yours,
"VIDA D. SCUDDER."

WHY DOES NOT THE CHURCH TURN SOCIALIST?[1]

A PERTINENT question! For according to the Church's formulæ one would have expected it to turn Socialist long ago. Wasn't it started Socialist? Did not its founder assert with vigor that an abundance of private possessions was bad and dangerous for a man? Did He not by deliberate choice announce His Good News to the poor, and establish principles that would make it impossible for any honest follower to fight for his own advantage, or to possess while other men lacked? Did He not go about proclaiming a revolutionary social order which He called the Kingdom of Heaven, and does not clear thinking show that socialism is the only economic basis which would ever give this ideal of His a thorough and fair chance? Finally, because He would not

[1] Reprinted from a Socialist publication, *The Coming Nation*, March, 1913.

give up his convictions or change His methods, did not the civil and religious authorities, with just instinct from their point of view, execute Him as a revolutionist and agitator?

Well, then! Why has his Church not turned out a revolutionary and Socialist body?

Your glib answer is ready to the question.

The Church is one thing, you say with a shrug: Jesus is quite another.

The Church does not turn Socialist because it is false to its Master; because ever since the time of Constantine it has flouted His ideas, misused His name, and has in these latter days at least, whatever may have been true earlier, become a stronghold of enmity to the people, and to the cause for which He died.

There is some force to this answer; but it is altogether too facile. Nothing in the world is so simple as all that. True, it does certainly look as if the Church might crucify Jesus all over again, did He appear among us. And we have to confess that it has crucified Him over and over, down the last two thousand years. Nevertheless, it still bears His name and includes many of His sincere followers.

The Church and the Hour

The situation demands that we probe deeper.

And the moment we do so we see that there is no use in pummeling the Church as if it were a person. Dealing the ecclesiastical world "slaps and slams" in the elegant phrase of a socialist contemporary is an easy and stimulating exercise, but a silly one; for there is really nothing around to be hit. The Church is an extremely complex proposition.

Seek for it with your sociological spy-glass, and it evades you. Which Church? Where? For the purposes of the present discussion, the Church cannot be considered as one corporate being endowed with independent life. Neither can it be identified with its leaders or official spokesmen, be they bishops or just plain ministers or even vestrymen and deacons. The Church is a vast association of baptized persons, presenting immense variety in outlook, attitude, and creed, held together by a force somewhat difficult to define.

This association has been in existence a long while and has lived through many social orders. It gets its color from these orders but it has never been identical with any of them;

in one way it has nothing to do with politics or sociology. It cannot officially turn socialist as a corporate body, any more than it could turn imperialist under the Roman Empire, or feudal under feudalism, or capitalistic under capitalism.

Partisanship in politics or economics is as much out of its corporate province as partisanship on these lines would be to a botanical association or a football team. The only way in which this association can turn Socialist is for the majority of the individuals composing it to turn Socialist; and this is what we really are watching for and are surprised not to see.

Now, the force that unites these individuals in the vital Church, the working Church, is the belief that they have something precious to guard. Brotherhood? Yes; but something also deeper and more sacred than brotherhood.

You may think that there is nothing deeper or more sacred. You may hold that brotherhood is the essence of religion, and all there is to it. You have a right to your opinion; but that is where good Christians, not to speak of good Buddhists, and Jews, and Mohammedans and Bahaists, differ from you.

This most precious thing which the Church exists to guard is the fellowship of finite and transitory man with Infinite and Uncreated Love.

Mystical delusion you say? Very well, though it seems somewhat unscientific to dismiss lightly with an impatient phrase an experience which has been from the dawn of time the central passion and the supreme desire, a sustaining power, a consolation, and a light, to unnumbered throngs of every continent and every tongue. Pure religious aspiration is intangible, but it is mighty. From land to land, from age to age, it may change its formulæ, but it never abandons its essence. And those who know can tell us that it never was more profoundly operative than to-day.

However, we are expounding just now—not attacking, or defending. And we hasten to add, for the benefit of the practically disposed, that this insistent craving for fellowship with the unseen is not the only factor in the bond that unites Church and people. It carries with it of necessity a further emphasis. For in the Church it is held that such fellowship can be attained only through growth in holiness.

Now, holiness is only another word for character raised to its highest possibilities.

It means in each individual a triumph of the higher nature over the lower, triumph won by fierce and endless moral struggle, of which the seat is the individual heart. The achievement of such triumph on the part of as many individuals as possible is the one matter of importance in the world. Hopelessly individualistic, you perceive. Still, the race does happen to be made up of individuals.

Even to appraise the value of an economic scheme, you have to get back to your individual every time. At all events, character is the word of the Church—involving on the lower levels morality or faithfulness to the law of right; on the higher levels, holiness, or unity with the law of love; and always implying the possibility, clouded, dim, yet infinitely precious, of fellowship with what lies beyond the world of sense.

The Church perceives or thinks she does that these things can be and are attained under all conceivable variety of economic circumstance; and therefore she is inclined not to care a rap whether people are rich or poor and whether they live in comfort or discomfort.

Even with the ethical stress, this whole scheme of things is foolishness to those moderns, if such there be, who hold that good housing conditions and adequate reward for every man are the omega as well as the alpha of human needs; also to those others, indubitably numerous, who are convinced that the study of natural law, with the pursuit of "arts yet unimagined yet to be" is going to satisfy the hunger for a vision of Truth beyond the edge of the world.

But these moderns must realize how ardently the people who fill the churches believe the other way. All church folk to whom religion is a reality speak a language of their own. They are sure that they, with any others who recognize the human need for that great fellowship with the Unseen God, alone "inhabit reality," to use James's admirable phrase. And the reason they do not turn socialist is their fear that socialism, especially as it is currently presented, threatens the power to achieve such fellowship.

They do not feel that people if released from economic bondage will be any more likely to become heirs to the old title, "Friends of God." They are full of terror lest a concentration of the public mind on the goods of the flesh should blind it to the goods of the Spirit; lest socialism should persuade men to a lazy idea that the race will be made good by rote when the socialist state arrives, and that meanwhile we fulfill our whole duty if we agitate for this state, relaxing all stress on the ancient tussle for individual self-restraint and goodness.

The religious world, so far as it holds aloof from socialism, inclines to one of two attitudes. Either it thinks that socialism offers a low substitute for religion, mere wheat bread for the Bread of Life, in which case it regards socialism as an enemy; or else it thinks as we were saying that economic circumstance bears no relation to character, in which case it regards socialism as irrelevant.

How full we are of answers—we Christians who happen to be socialists! The present writer has recently written a whole book to prove to her fellow-Christians how wrong they are. We are in a hurry to say that the Food of Immortality can be sacramentally conveyed only through common bread and wine; that in the blessed oneness of being, soul helps flesh "no more than flesh helps soul," so that our plain business is to make the flesh of all men healthful and wholesome; and we point with horror to the Satanic forces of Disease and Apathy brooding sinister over factory and slum.

I am afraid that we socialist Christians enjoy hearing St. James say to the capitalists, especially those who fill the churches: Go to now, weep and howl! Certainly we hold with John that if a man does not love his brother whom he has seen he is not likely to love God whom he has not seen; and just as we perceive (what many good people curiously fail to) that the brotherhood of man implies Fatherhood—somewhere—so we see that a universal Fatherhood implies a brotherhood not of our seeking but of divine ordaining.

Probably a majority of people in the churches now get as far as this. There is a quite general loathing of self-centered spirituality to-day and a strong reaction from nursing our own souls while babies are making artificial flowers. And a significant minority gets further. It sees that socialism is the only effective way at this stage of social evolution of practicing human fellowship, and so reaching fellowship with God.

This minority in the Church is very firm in its conviction. It is quite sure that faith in Dante's "Love that moves the sun and the other stars" is in the long run the only asset that separates man from brute; but it is also equally sure that socialism will prove favorable to the full expansion of such faith and that the socialist reorganization of society is the only way to give the endless struggle for the perfecting of individual character, which is the condition of spiritual vision, any kind of a fair show.

We try our best to show this to all our fellow-Christians. But still they hesitate. Still they tell us that there is danger lest the precious things attained by blood and tears and anguish be all thrown away, lest moral freedom be abolished by our system, and the race sink back into a dreary vulgarity, a kind of ethical Philistinism, with no romance of the spirit, no fine heroisms, no more quest for the light that glimmers at the horizon's verge.

Their fears sound plausible. We must do justice to their honesty: to that jealous, serious passion for moral and spiritual values which is in great part the source of the difficulty felt by religious people in accepting Socialism.

We of the minority can hardly refrain from retorting, however, that if economic comfort be a dangerous condition, or an irrelevant one, it is strange that church members should for the most part cling to it so tenaciously—and possess so very large a share of it, compared with the babies making artificial flowers.

Honest church people have an interesting answer ready. They have to grant us something, and they point to St. Francis, or to his theories, and tell us that we are right in a degree, but that the way out is not to press socialism but to persuade them and their like to a voluntary sacrifice of their possessions.

Now there is a great deal to be said about this answer which cannot be said to-day. But it certainly does sound just a little academic and Utopian—and the babies continue to starve. Meantime it points us to other factors in the situation less noble than those we have been considering, yet important to keep in mind if we are looking for a straight answer to our question.

The Church has that inward life on which we have been dwelling. But it has an outward life also. And this outward life is largely dependent on the offerings of the well-to-do classes. It is certainly a far cry from Fifth Avenue ecclesiastical architecture to the shores of the Lake of Galilee; yet by natural process of growth, Fifth Avenue Church edifices have appeared.

The Church is an institution maintaining buildings and officials and an enormous quantity of charitable work, excellently well meant, however shortsighted. Now the inward life is by far the deeper and more important. It is what holds the whole thing together. Were it conceivable that the craving for union with God should cease in the hearts of men, the Church would vanish within a generation. All the handsome church buildings, the vested choirs, the eloquent preachers, the full congregations, would "like the cloudy fabric of a vision leave not a rack behind," if once the race lost sight of that faint gleam—on the clouds is it? Or shining from a land very far off, beyond the confines of sense? But so long as that craving endures, churches will be built,—and perhaps the building of them will always hurt and hamper the freedom of the exploring mind.

The paradox of the situation reacts painfully on the hearts of church people, especially of officials. How can they imperil their hold on the community which supports the Church and all its works, by joining forces with those who would menace the very basis on which that community rests? It is not in most cases a crude question with clergymen of retaining their jobs, though this consideration has to come in; it is rather a question of the enterprises which they father. And there are many drawn to the Socialist faith who, for one or the other reason, do not dare to join us.

At least three clergymen of good standing in their respective communions have avowed this to the writer within the year. "Wait till I educate my children," said one. "I do not wish to lose the power for good, and indirectly for socialism, which I now exert through an academic chair," said the second. "You see," sighed the third, "we carry on schools, and if I were to join the socialist party, those schools would be ruined."

Lamentable enough. Yet even in these cases the reasons for hesitation were not wholly ignoble. Mere counsels of prudence and timidity would never have prevailed with these honest and devoted men.

Further conversation revealed the strong feeling in all of them,—and it is a feeling very wide-spread,— that while socialism was doubtless the true economic doctrine, the socialist movement in America was too materialistic, autocratic, and quarrelsome for churchmen to join without endorsing a spirit which they were bound to disapprove. The confusion of motive was very bad for them, and for us.

What to do about the situation? Well, we are not concerned to-day with answers,-- and my space is gone.

One trouble is that Nature expects us to be enthusiastic about a number of things at once, and we all find it hard to obey. We cannot respond to the amplitude of her demands.

We do not manage half as well as Humpty Dumpty in *Alice*, who had trained himself to believe as many as ten impossible things before breakfast; we can hardly ever believe more than one at a time. Nature herself does many things all at once, but when she desires to get a piece of work done by men, says Emerson somewhere, she evolves a type of people who feel that the achievement of that one end is the only thing which matters in the universe.

So orthodox church people, believing intensely that the growth of the soul is the only important thing, find it hard not to distrust the socialists, who so hate cant about the soul that they never mention the organ. Orthodox socialists meanwhile, thinking it supremely important that babies should not make artificial flowers, find it hard not to be a little contemptuous of people who stay aloof from the great modern struggle for economic freedom.

Yet there is no logical reason why socialists should not care for spiritual values, and religious people care for social justice. There is every reason why they should, for the indications are that Nature has both at heart, and that neither cause can in the long run flourish without the other. Perhaps socialists and Christians alike will learn this some day. So far as the Church is concerned, there is always that strong and growing minority. Give us time.

In England, they say that the advance of socialism depends largely on the church vote. Ten more years here in the United States, and who knows what may happen? Especially if socialists should get more in the habit of acknowledging that the soul is of importance.

A PLEA FOR SOCIAL INTERCESSION

EVERYONE knows that religion is undergoing a social revival. Where our fathers agonized over sins of the inner man, we lament our social crimes. Where they analyzed their relations to God, we analyze our relations to our brothers. Perhaps we are less conscious than the Puritans were of loving Him whom no man hath seen at any time,—but we are a great deal more conscious of loving our fellow-men.

The change of attitude may entail loss as well as gain. If it means pragmatic indifference to the things of the spirit, it means loss. If it means that anything, however lovely and sacred, supplants in the soul the supreme desire for the Living God, it cuts life at the heart-root, and though the plant may still seem green and fresh for a time, slow death is on the way. There is reason to fear that modern social feeling does have these bad tendencies sometimes. The quest for union with Eternal Love is a stern and fearsome thing, and men are always seeking facile substitutes. So they try to replace this quest by a vague humanitarian ardor, press the sure truth that *laborare est orare* to the point of eliminating *orare* altogether, and make a religion out of ministering to the poor and working for social justice. When they feel the need for more contemplation, as everybody does at times, they betake them if they can to the great woods and relax pleasantly as they enjoy Nature. These people are repeating in modern fashion the specious error of the old "Quietists," whom Ruysbroek so dreaded in the fourteenth century. For they are without that "eternal hunger which shall never more be satisfied; it is an inward craving and hankering of the loving power and the created spirit after an uncreated Good." "Fruitive love," which is the old mystic's final phrase for the ideal life, is denied to them: Instead of this, they "enter into rest through mere nature . . . and this rest may be found and possessed within themselves by all creatures, without the grace of God. . . .

In this bare vacancy, the rest is pleasant and great." . . . "This rest is in itself no sin," says Ruysbroek, but it has no relation to "the supernatural rest which one possesses in God." However much such people may be addicted to good works, they can never, he says. enter the arcana.

A condition like this is lamentable and superficial. Yet no one would lose out from religion that intense social preoccupation which is now seizing on it. For a mighty force is regenerating the whole body of the Church. The recovery of social emphasis in the spiritual life is the great means by which our age is getting "back to Christ," who in nearly all His teachings was primarily concerned with mens' relations to one another. We can pray the Lord's Prayer as it has not been prayed since the days of the Master, and we are learning the force of the sequence in the petitions. "Hallowed be Thy Name": the attainment of a lofty, holy, hallowed conception of God is humanity's first need. "Thy Kingdom come, Thy will be done, on earth": the coming of the Kingdom, the true social order over which God can reign unchallenged and supreme, precedes the doing of the Will, which is the personal, intimate fulfillment, of the Divine life within. And then, descending to the present level from that aspiration toward ultimate ideals which prayer must never forfeit or postpone, the petitions for immediate needs. "Give us THIS DAY our daily bread": let all humanity receive the physical nourishment which it requires. "Forgive as we forgive,"—we are negatively indulgent enough sometimes toward sinners but do we forgive them quite as we want God to forgive us? "Lead us not into temptation, deliver us from evil,"—and our whole industrial system adapted it would seem almost deliberately to tempt the strong and to betray the weak! The great petitions are a social program in themselves, which if we live as we pray will carry us far indeed toward expressing the Mind of Christ in a new order of Christian living.

No, we cannot give up our social vision and we may not give up our ancient quest. Rightly understood, each fulfills the other. And in one special way they meet. It is the Way of Prayer, modeled on the Prayer of

The Church and the Hour

the Lord, the Way of Intercession. Through intercession, the old type of religion is one with the new, and aspiration rises Godward even while tenderness holds humanity in its embrace.

Intercession is the counterpart in the life within of social work in the life without. Of all effective work it is the soul. In vain does the Church create social service commissions, and announce fairly drastic programs of social reform. In vain does the community establish associations to fight every evil under the sun, organize efficient relief for its social victims, and grope toward new industrial ideals. All this is good, and one rejoices that whatever a man's tastes and convictions, there is a place for him in the social crusade. It is good, it is necessary; but at times it all turns to ashes in the mouth. We look abroad, and "brothers" in the awkward words of a well-meaning hymn, are still "engaging." We look at home, and we know that nobody is living as St. Francis would live, or St. John. Are we, for that matter, living as Jesus would have us live? Here is a graver question: whose conscience is wholly free? Futility and helplessness press us down. In the night-silence, our fussy energies seem pretty poor things, pretty useless.

And all the while we have power—sure power—power that goes straight to the mark. Truly, truly, Christ says to us, Whatsoever ye ask in My Name, I will do it.

Whatsoever! And what are we asking? Let us examine our prayers. How languid they are, how perfunctory, and alas! how often selfish! Sometimes one feels that men's prayers must sadden God even more than their sins. Prayer is the deepest and surest measure of personality. As men pray, so they really are. For people do pray even in these unbelieving days for what they want intensely. When a dear friend is in peril, they pray. When they encounter personal crisis, they pray. When they see a glorious sunset, they instinctively lift their hearts to the Source of Light. But prayer must be more than instinct or sudden emotion, it must be the habit of the disciplined Christian life. A force more penetrating and powerful than gravitation or electricity is entrusted to us, and we are responsible for the steady use of it and its direction to the noblest ends. Do men look to wide horizons, do they ask great things? Or is their inward life self-centered even while the outer may be filled with fine impersonal interests? If they really want social justice they will pray for it; activities are not worth much unless they constantly turn into upward-leaping desire.

Some people think themselves religious just because they like to pray and to go to church. And of course that is something, but it is not very much. To spend our precious time for prayer,—usually scant at best, —in begging for personal gifts and graces, or in enjoyment of personal consolations is as selfish as to spend active lives in pursuit of personal gain, and one can be as greedy in spiritual affairs as in any others. The time can go in asking for health or wealth or success or affection or pleasure or peace; it can go in asking similar gifts for friends, which is very much better. But do most people get farther than their own circle? Does their prayer reveal that the rescue of children from wage-slavery, of men from conditions that stifle manhood, of women from the manifold evils which weigh them down, is a potent and passionate desire? Prayer is the desire most native to the soul turned Godward, and egotism at the center of the soul's life is an awful thing.

It is the impression of such egotism conveyed by the life of many mystics and holy men, which has caused, often unjustly, the reaction against them. But how great, how subtle, the danger! The best way of escaping it without running into the opposite danger is the practice of intercession. For by intercession, life at the center, life in the sanctuary, may be purified from self and lost that it may be found. Also, life is energized; for right praying involves hard thinking, and the mind addicted to indolent evasion will never kindle the sacred fire. God sets no limit to audacious importunity. Men may ask for the greatest things, for the industrial and political peace of the world, for universal justice. But if their prayers are to prevail, they must avoid all lazy generalizations, they must have point and precision of aim. In proportion as they attain breadth, point, and ardor, the hidden life turned inward will be cleansed from selfishness and the life turned outward from arrogance or discouragement, and the kingdom will come faster than men dream.

There is secret sacrifice involved in placing special emphasis on Intercession. It is the sacrifice demanded by an age peculiarly called to labor for social ideals. Petition at highest is only a small part of prayer. Praise is a blessed duty, confession of sin a necessity: above all other forms comes that pure single concentrated Practise of the Presence of God whence flows all peace and power. Considering the richness of the life hid with Christ in God through prayer, one cannot marvel if it drew men of old away from all earthly pursuits to an exclusive consecration. But the Via Contemplativa is to-day the way for very few; and perhaps precisely in the sacrifice of dearer energies, the subordination of possible hidden joys, lies part of our expiation for communal guilt. The joys may wait on that great day when the redeemed of the Lord shall come to Zion with songs and with everlasting joy upon their heads. Here and now, God may best be found by those who in the secret life forever deny in part even their higher desires, that they may lift the sorrowful needs of the world up to his Heart of Mercy.

Through intercession, the handicapped, the sick, the feeble, the inhibited from action, can find their place, can march shoulder to shoulder with the vigorous, or perhaps can lead the march, in the inspiriting advance toward the Kingdom of Justice. Legislative reforms, and greater things, may be achieved by desires rising from some obscure bed of pain. Yet this is no mere work for private initiative, it is also a work for the Church. Men grope to discover how an aroused Christian community can react on the social situation through its ecclesiastical machinery; the answer is difficult, opinions vary. Some say that the clergy should throw themselves into politics, some that they should stay out. Some want institutional churches, some despise them. Some wish the Church to inaugurate social service under her own name, others think that if she does she will simply chip in at cross purposes to wiser secular agencies. But one thing the churches surely can do without harming or interfering,—they can summon people to pray for social justice, and they can teach them how. In a parish or a diocese, or in the Church universal, why should not a Novena or a Week of Prayer be now and then proclaimed against some shocking evil —child labor, or the White Slave traffic? If Christian people threw themselves heartily and reverently into such a scheme and got themselves ready for prayer by becoming intelligent on the issue, what an access to zeal would ensue on the merely human side! And in that unseen region whither prayers wing their flight, who can tell what forces would be set in motion?

Phillips Brooks used to tell how a number of good Episcopalians got together at the time of the great Boston fire and said the Litany. "And there was a provision in it for everything under the sun," said he, "except for a burning city." Obviously, this special Church has been sadly in need of more flexibility, and she has been gaining it lately. Intercession services are common and increasingly prized. Cannot they be more vigorously turned toward social salvation, while losing none of their fervor for missions, for parochial ends, for individual needs? Will not the numerous Guilds of Prayer develop social intercession? One such guild at least is especially pledged to pray for the reconciliation of classes, and so, whenever a great strike or labor war is in progress, hundreds of people all over the country are entreating, with what ardor God and their conscience vouchsafe, not that one side or the other may triumph necessarily, but that brotherhood may prevail.

Yet there is no need to wait for corporate action. Let every man examine his private life. Is he satisfied with the idea God gains of him from his prayers? In prayer more than in any other pursuit one must be honest; there is danger in pretending to desire what one does not really care about. But also one may grow. The world-crisis calls men faithfully and fervently to enlarge and energize their life of prayer. So the old and the new ideals of religious life will be brought into unison; so the Mystical Body of Christ will come to her own, in power to help and heal. Thank God for letting us pray! May we be worthy of the Gift and the Summons!

THE SIGN OF THE SON OF MAN

Thy Kingdom, Lord, we long for,
　　Where love shall find its own,
And brotherhood triumphant
　　Our years of pride disown.
Thy captive people languish
　　In mill and mart and mine;
We lift to Thee their anguish,
　　We wait Thy promised Sign!

Thy Kingdom, Lord, Thy Kingdom,
　　All secretly it grows;
In faithful hearts forever
　　His seed the Sower sows.
Yet ere its consummation
　　Must dawn a mighty doom.
For judgment and salvation
　　The Son of Man shall come.

The Church and the Hour

If now perchance in tumult
   His destined Sign appear,—
The Rising of the People,—
   Dispel our coward fear!
Let comforts that we cherish,
   Let old tradition die;
Our wealth, our wisdom perish,
   So that He draw but nigh!

In wrath and revolution
   The Sign may be displayed,
But by Thy grace we'll greet it
   With spirits unafraid.
The awestruck heart presages
   An Advent dread and sure;
It hails the hope of ages—
   Its Master in the poor.

Beyond our fierce confusions,
   Our strife of speech and sword,
Our wars of class and nation,
   We wait Thy certain Word.

The meek and poor in spirit
  Who in Thy promise trust
The Kingdom shall inherit,
  The blessing of the Just.

THE END

www.ingramcontent.com/pod-product-compliance
Lightning Source LLC
Chambersburg PA
CBHW050829160426
43192CB00010B/1957